The Power of Change

Reinventing Yourself at Any Age

Edited by Linda Ellis Eastman

Professional Woman Publishing
Prospect, Kentucky

The Power of Change: Reinvent Yourself at Any Age

Published by:
Professional Woman Publishing
Post Office Box 333
Prospect, KY 40059
(502) 228-0906
www.pwnbooks.com

Please contact the publisher for quantity discounts.

ISBN 13: 978-0-9845827-7-8
ISBN 10: 0-9845827-7-0

Library of Congress Cataloging-In-Publication Data

Cover Design and Typography by:
Sential Design, LLC — www.sentialdesign.com
Photo credits: irinaqqq/Dreamstime

Printed in the United States of America

Dedicated to Tricia Stoddard for her vision to step from aeronautical engineer to becoming an educator in Compton, California. She is a reminder that no matter our age, we can follow our passion and vision.

Table of Contents

Table of Contents
—Continued—

Table of Contents
—Continued—

ABOUT THE AUTHOR

LINDA ELLIS EASTMAN

Linda Ellis Eastman is President and CEO of The Professional Woman Network (PWN), an International Training and Consulting Organization on Women's Issues. She has designed seminars which have been presented in China, the former Soviet Union, South Africa, the Phillipines, and attended by individuals in the United States from such firms as McDonalds, USA Today, Siemens-Westinghouse, the Pentagon, the Department of Defense, and the United States Department of Education.

An expert on women's issues, Ms. Eastman has certified and trained over two thousand women to start consulting/seminar businesses originating from such countries as Pakistan, the Ukraine, Antigua, Canada, Mexico, Zimbabwe, Nigeria, Bermuda, Jamaica, Costa Rica, England, South Africa, Malaysia, and Kenya. Founded in 1982 by Linda Ellis Eastman, The Professional Woman Network is committed to educating women on a global basis regarding, self-esteem, confidence building, stress management, and emotional, mental, spiritual and physical wellness.

Ms. Eastman has been featured in USA Today and listed in Who's Who of American Women, as well as Who's Who of International Leaders. In addition to women's issues, Ms. Eastman speaks internationally regarding the importance of human respect as it relates to race, color, culture, age, and gender. She will be facilitating an international conference where speakers and participants from many nations will be able to discuss issues that are unique to women on a global basis.

Linda Ellis Eastman is also founder of The Professional Woman Speakers Bureau and The Professional Woman Coaching Institute. Ms. Eastman has dedicated her businesses to increasing the self-esteem and personal dignity of women and youth around the world.

Contact:
The Professional Woman Network
P.O. Box 333
Prospect, KY 40059
(502) 566-9900
lindaeastman@prodigy.net
www.pwnbooks.com
www.protrain.net

Introduction

Linda Ellis Eastman

No matter a woman's circumstance, she has the ability to change from within and recreate her life and start over again. Whether she is faced with a difficult divorce, a verbally abusive boss at work, a chronic illness that has changed her lifestyle, or self-doubt, the power of a woman to overcome is evident in history.

Consider Rosa Parks who was courageous and challenged the norm in the United States by her insistence to not succumb to second-class treatment. Diane Sawyer, news anchor, was open about depression and bi-polar disorder thus helping to change the perception of mental illness. And let us not forget autistic Dr. Temple Grandin who chose to rise to the top of her profession in creating new guidelines for the humane treatment of animals. These women not only changed themselves, they helped change the world.

No matter your age, you have the power to search deep within and reflect upon what really matters to you. Step into your own strength to challenge that which in unfair in the world or to look closely into your inner 'mirror' and change personal behaviors and thinking that sabotage your own personal success and confidence.

Within your own family or circle of friends, there may be a woman (or girl!) who has stepped forward and garnered the strength to challenge the norm. You know someone who has changed her own life by overcoming addictions or walked (or run) away from an abusive relationship. They have chosen to reinvent their own lives.

You have the power to do the same.

The Power of Change

Reinventing Yourself at Any Age

ABOUT THE AUTHOR

SHIRLEY A. WILLIAMS

Shirley A. William is President and CEO of ***Leadership in Action, LLC***. Her mission is "Developing the workforce of today to meet the needs of tomorrow". She conducts workshops and seminars that have been presented throughout the United States and abroad. The workshops and seminars conducted by the institute consist of topics such as: Women as Leaders, Leadership Skills and The Superwoman Syndrome. Ms. Williams has been certified by The Professional Woman Network as a Professional Coach and Diversity Consultant.

Ms. Williams' knowledge of business and professionalism is supported by over 20 years of real world and practical leadership experience acquired from the telecom and staffing industries, non-profit, university and faith based organizations. She has over 12 years experience in employee recognition, training recruiting, and change and knowledge management.

Among her many accomplishments, Ms. Williams has co-authored 9 PNW books and her first solo book to be released in the fall of 2011. She has been recognized by the Lydia Circle of Christian Business and Professional Women with the ***Spirit of Deborah Leadership Award*** and ***Leadership Advancement Award***.

Books

- Co-Author of "***The Baby Boomer's Handbook For Women***" (August 2008)

Certifications

- Certified Professional Coach
- Registered Corporate Coach
- Certified Diversity Consultant
- Certified DISC Behavior Model Consultant

Professional Spotlight

- The Magnolia Radio Show, Baby Boomer's Handbook for Women "***Reinventing Yourself at Any Age***" (August 2008)

Professional Organizations

- Professional Woman's Speakers Bureau
- Professional Woman's Authors Institute and board Member
- National Association of Female Executives
- Lydia Circle of Christian Business and Professional Women
- National Association of Baby Boomer Women
- ASTD (Association of Training and Development)

Contact:
Shirley A. Williams
P.O. Box 3238, Southfield, MI 48037
(888) 926-9911
www.leadershipinaction.info
swilliams@leadershipinaction.info

ONE

Stop The Drama! Living Your Life Without Chaos

By Shirley A. Williams

"All I'm saying is simply this, that all life is interrelated, that somehow we're caught in an inescapable network of mutuality tied in a single garment of destiny. Whatever affects one directly affects all indirectly. For some strange reason, I can never be what I ought to be until you are what you ought to be. You can never be what you ought to be until I am what I ought to be. This is the interrelated structure of reality."

—Dr. Martin Luther King Jr.

I work faithfully at staying out of the line of fire when it comes to drama. I like to keep myself positioned in an atmosphere that promotes peace over unrest, confusion and drama and order over chaos and disorder. From the time I was a young girl it was always my desire to travel through life with a calm and peaceful temperament. In fact, I do all that I can to limit my exposure to drama-filled environments and the people who accept and embrace the turmoil, unruliness and disruption and the sheer madness that comes along with it. I understand that there is some drama and some chaos that we cannot avoid during our lifetimes like the loss of a loved one or a job, illnesses and accidents that occur. Although events such as those happen, we continue to hope, pray and believe that they are temporary; and we trust that any residual negative feelings we hold in our hearts will change with time and the appropriate actions and a fresh look at the situation.

My life is challenging enough without incorporating all of the unnecessary drama that unfortunately belongs to other people. Because of the relationships we have with these people we find ourselves giving ourselves permission to become victims of their volatile and conflicted world. We go along with their drama for a while and then for even a while longer because of our sense of loyalty toward them until we open our eyes and acknowledge the effect and the toll that their stuff has on our lives. This is the reason we have to limit our time around them. Let's face it, it is already becoming more challenging to remain positive during these chaotic times that we are experiencing in the world today. Striving to be an "up" person in an upside down world can be very exhausting when drama, chaos and the disorder it generates in our lives comes at us on every front. I can clearly see all of the confusion, unrest and disrespect it can cause looking at it from a spectator's point of view on my life. It is a very troubling picture to see. Reality shows, politicians, religious leaders, celebrities, athletes and others that we once aspired to be like have also contributed to the polarization of the drama and chaotic way of life in our culture today. Our momentary look into the often over-exaggerated window of their drama-filled dysfunctional lives has somehow become a model that we have embraced as a lifestyle to be celebrated. Our obsession with reality shows is evidence of this as an entertaining theory. To think that we find all of this as an entertaining and acceptable way of life in our society today is disheartening. What's even more mind-boggling for me is how some of us crave this kind of drama. I suppose we thrive on their messiness so much because it excuses us from acknowledging our own self-destructive behavior and satisfies our voyeuristic need for excitement that we feel we might be missing out on in our own lives. We will never admit to ourselves that we can also get caught into playing the role of drama queen or king. However, there are times when we find great pleasure in hanging out at the playground called mayhem and involving ourselves in play dates with all of our friends who are teammates in the game of pandemonium. Whatever the case may be, this might be why we are so hasty and willing to invite the commotion it brings with it into our homes, workplaces, playgrounds, politics in our schools and our personal and public communities at large. The drama queens and kings find pleasure in dragging us into their madness and pulling us into the mud with them. Every now and then, we are more than willing to go along with them since they can spot us drama magnets anywhere. For the sake of acceptance and validation we straddle the fence, sending mixed messages about our interest in being a participant because we find it amusing to see how much mayhem they can stir up, especially when we find that we are not their focal point for confrontation or competition.

Think about this scenario for a moment: if a stranger entered your life to spend a couple of weeks with you, your family, at your job and in your circle of friends, what impression of you would this stranger take away with them? Would you be perceived as a drama advocate, drama magnet or a drama free promoter who is not interested in dealing with or having anything to do with someone that encourages or thrives on drama? Would you be viewed as someone they would possibly want to eliminate from their list of people to continue a relationship with? Are you the person they can delete from their list because your drama is getting old and does nothing to enrich their life? What would your list look like if I were to challenge you to close your eyes for a moment and come up with an image of someone in your life circle that comes to mind when you hear the words confusion, unorganization, out-of-control, extreme behavior, door-slammer, shouting, fist pounding and excessively emotional. The face you might see is the person who becomes highly agitated with things as small as traffic jams, paper jams at work or jam spilling on the floor at home. Can you see their face? Is it yours? I imagine you will have no problem coming up with a few names. Who's face did you see and how many faces came to mind? Now, if you are serious about identifying the drama advocates in your life, I suggest that as you concentrate on the people in your circle of life you will include yourself in the assessment, as well. Take a look in the mirror and ask yourself: is it me? Take a moment here and make a list of the people that cause you and others to tense up at just the sound of their name. Reflect on the people that can clear a room the moment their name is mentioned because so much tension fills the air, because of the fact that everyone knows they are bringing their drama with them. As you write the names on paper, or just make a mental note, ask yourself what their drama is and why does it matter to you? Examine the names you listed and search inside for the reasons those people popped into your mind and then ask yourself if you, in any way, have knowingly or unknowingly acted as a co-conspirator in their theater of madness? If you were on a committee that had to select a poster child to be a symbol of drama and chaos would the names of those you selected be an undeniable choice in the eyes of others, as well? At this point, ask yourself this last question: how does the drama and chaos of this relationship help to enhance your quality of life? If you come to the conclusion that their drama will not add any value to your life, you may want to consider how you can change the dynamic of the relationship so each of you can get what you need from it. Be honest with them and let them know that you value the relationship; however, it is sometimes stressful for you and it makes you uncomfortable. Make it plain to them that you do not like the antics or the "cloud of chaos" that often infiltrates a room when they arrive. Try to make them aware of the uneasiness you subject yourself to when this occurs and that you no longer want to be in included in these activities.

Over the past several years I have found that I have been asking myself more and more frequently why it is necessary for me to tolerate the unnecessary drama. I have come to a point where I recognize that life is too precious to waste time on the dumb stuff. I don't know about you but what I do know about myself is that I am looking to invest my time in people that add value to my life by seeing the positive and looking for ways to minimize the drama, chaos and negativity. I want people around me that add to or represent a plus-point, not people who subtract, take away or waste those precious moments from my life with their drama and nonsense. I choose and want to be surrounded by people who make me laugh, encourage me and lift my spirits. I prefer to limit the time I give to those who are constantly throwing a whiny pity-party for themselves, tossing their drama and chaos in the air like confetti.

The drama advocates that I have bumped into over the course of my life remind me of a stalker who has a way of finding you wherever you live, work or play. Their sole purpose appears to be persuading you to endorse, carry and advance the drama. They want you to help them take the drama to their final destination which is a place called chaos.

The following quote, often referred to as "the butterfly effect", is a saying often used in connection with describing chaos,

"A butterfly flapping its wings in one part of the world can cause a hurricane on the other side of the Earth."

It is not uncommon for chaos to be on the heels of drama. Drama has the ability to activate a chain reaction that can change the environment and the people in its path forever. For me "Dramaville" is not a place I like to visit often because many of its agents, the drama queens and kings that I have encountered, only seem to thrive in an extreme state of confusion; that their mere presence creates. For those of you who think you do not know any drama kings or queens let me describe them for you so that it might help you recognize them when they show up. They would be the person that can magnify or amplify a situation or a story by using theatrics and their excessive behavior and can be magnified by 300%. They are skilled at increasing your anxiety and anger levels, they can cause your heart rate to increase and they leave you feeling that someone has sucked the life out of you if you let them. Everything in their world is more urgent than anything could possibly be in your unimportant world because their bottom line is; everything is about them and the stuff in your life is small in comparison. For instance, a person could have Cancer, yet their broken fingernail is more devastating in their world. The core of their existence is their ability to tap into the counterfeit theatrical and or artificial bag of emotions that comes with their drama.

When the occasion arises for me to come co-mingle with the drama queens or kings I have no problem letting them know right up front that I am on a "drama-free and reduced chaos diet." From a health standpoint (mind, body and soul) I have learned over the years that operating with this mind set is in my best interest. I also keep myself surrounded with positive people who also like the peace we feel when we settle on a drama-free environment and way of life. Rejecting the drama, histrionics and theatrics reduces my stress levels, eliminates the confusion and disorder that is generated by the drama and prevents any given situation from getting out of control.

In all honesty, the only drama that I am interested in comes equipped with a small box and a remote control offering a wide selection of program choices. If I feel that the story line I happen to be watching at the time lacks the content I need, I just change the channel. I actually love that I have the option to change the channel when I want; choosing the program that meets my specific entertainment needs. Speaking of which, entertainment in my mind is something that brings me pleasure and not the theatrics that typically accompany the drama that is frequently overwhelming for some of us in real life. For most of my life I have attempted to fly under the radar when it comes to engaging in or getting drawn into the drama scene. Unfortunately when it comes to real life drama and the drama queens and kings starring in the story, it looks as if some thrive on the reruns of their negative memories and past. Even when they know that the story is not as bleak as it has been painted, rewriting the ending is never an option because the drama is more exciting. I have also noticed that we tend to give these people a pass on the occasions when their actions cause us hurt, pain or humiliation. I can even hear my voice from the past saying, "You know how they are," or, "That's just the way they are."

ABOUT THE AUTHOR

Joyce Murphy Hash

Mrs. Joyce Murphy Hash is a woman of God-called, appointed and anointed to carry out the work of the ministry. She is the faithful wife of Dr. James C. Hash, Sr. the Pastor of St. Peter's World Outreach Center, in Winston-Salem, North Carolina. Together, they serve a thriving congregation of 22 years in the ministry.

Mrs. Hash, a native of Wytheville, VA attended Victory Bible Institute in Tulsa, Oklahoma to further her spiritual training. God has richly blessed her with a profound capacity to feel compassion for every woman. She has a deeply intuitive nature, which the Holy Spirit prompts to discern issues of the soul and the spirit of women through the "InTouch Ladies Ministry", a ministry that leads the today's woman to reach her full potential by cultivating their own uniqueness and to know who she is no matter what her role in life is through mentorship and discipleship.

Her sincere caring, coupled with great wisdom, makes her an outstanding asset to her husband, her family, her church family, and the Body of Christ. Married forty-eight plus years, she and her husband have four beautiful children and nine wonderful grandchildren. Mrs. Hash places great emphasis on keeping balance and harmony in the home and providing loving support to the family.

Contact:
3683 Old Lexington Road
Winston-Salem, NC 27107
336.650.0200
jmhash@spwoc.com
www,spwoc.com

TWO

Your Personal DNA

By Lady Joyce Hash

Merriam Webster's dictionary defines change and reinvention as follows:

Change – to give a different position, cause, or direction.

Reinvention – to remake or redo completely.

The ability and power to change and reinvent oneself is essentially a concentrated effort of one to focus on their own DNA. We definitively know DNA to be Deoxyribonucleic Acid which is the hereditary material in humans. However, in one's plight and discovery I believe that it is important for each to find their own "DNA" which is:

D – Discover yourself

N – Nurture Wellness

A – Adjust your attitude

In discovering your new DNA it is essential that you focus on these three key elements:

1. Continually let go of the past.
2. Establish a sincere relationship with God.
3. Place yourself in a new and healthy environment that will support the new changes.

Letting Go of the Past

We constantly hear that we must move on from the different hurts and disappointments that we experience. But how does one really heal from traumatic situations like divorce or the passing of a loved one? How do we move on from these hurts and transition to the next phase of our lives? To move into the future one has to make the decision to daily and continually let go of the past. The process of making this decision can be hindered by many types of interference and distraction. Throughout this process we have to realize only we can change ourselves! These life situations can and will leave us vulnerable to the continual reopening of the wounds of the matter in its gripping powers the unforgiving darkness can creep in and cage no one in bondage but you. Yes you! The evil intentions of the past are to haunt our consciousness with the pains of yesterday. Each woman is different. Each woman has her own path to resolving her past pains and my path lead me to Christ. The more I searched for answers and the more I looked to other people I ended up becoming more vulnerable to confusion and despair. Thus, we all must make a solid decision and believe that tomorrow is a brighter day. Yesterday is gone. We can be healed from its memory.

The oppressions of yesterday, a traumatic childhood and tumultuous teenage years left me in destitute and despair with nowhere to turn. Reflection will lead one to make some of the biggest decisions of their lives. For me, I had to be willing to let all of those things go to have a new life. That decision and that choice of path will empower anyone to discover a new self. There is a great need for balance in our beings that we must acknowledge through the establishment of a relationship with God. This relationship acknowledges the superiority of His power. Only He can give the power to overcome and succeed in a life that often lures one into dwelling on the past. The trappings of yesterday with today's promise of victory gave hope that with a heart of faith and perseverance-the light would be sought and seen again. This, in turn, gave assurance that change like this can happen at any age.

Turning the corner from yesterday and transitioning into today can and enlighten and shift anyone from a life of external blame, or the blame of all around you, and bring you into a place of-introspection and focus. This enlightenment and shifting will not lead one to be introspective to a point of being self-centered or selfish, but to an internal realization that yesterday's trappings distracted you from the right and healthy focus of a healthy relationship with yourself. Years of hurt almost did not allow anyone the opportunity to get to know the true me.

Yesterday will keep you blind from seeing your true self. The darkness of pain, grief, hurt and a lack of forgiveness blinds a person from their authentic self. The loving arms of God led me to a place of a transparent awareness of the need to nurture a relationship with those around me, and most importantly, myself.

Psalms 51:1 - "Make Zion the place you delight in, repair Jerusalem's broken-down walls."

Discovery

<u>Discovery</u> – a different position, cause or direction; the definition of a complete makeover.

All of mankind has the abundant right to take and make a complete change or turn around to reinvent oneself. As mentioned before, the past and all the darkness attached to it can keep you in desperate need of repair, in a place of broken walls. All too often, especially as women, we are not aware of how life's issues have left us not only broken and in destitute, but in major need of repair. This different position, this enlightenment of brokenness, coupled with the acknowledgement of God, will lead you to the place of discovery of life and all of its new profound meaning. With God and His infinite power you have the inherit right to tap into his divinity and completely internally, as well externally, change into the person that you desire to be. A life that was once full of regrets will turn into a life with no regret. A life with no finances or resources will turn to a life of abundant resources and supplies. A life with no love will become a life of a new person who loves themselves and others with the ability to have a loved one in return who will love the entire, total new you! Infinite possibilities resides in and around you. Life and death will both abide in your tongue. For years, wrong messages and wrong words derailed our new existences and, in turn, we had to eat the fruit thereof. But, with our new discovery we can and will reframe a new life. You have the power to change -absolutely no one but you. You are the new CEO of your destiny. Your new encouragement and positivity have empowered you for your new self. Let's take the time right now and say these declarations to the new and improved self:

- I have a new fresh start!
- I am created anew!
- My tongue is an instrument of life, not death.
- I speak words of love and affirmation to myself and others.
- My old life is behind me.
- No more sorrows of yesterday.
- A new beautiful life beckons me and I respond to it.
- I discover life and its new meaning!
- Before me stands a beautiful and whole woman.
- I embrace my new life, right NOW!
- I am a new woman all around through and through.

Nurture Wellness

Ephesians 4:23-24 (The Message): "A life renewed from the inside. And working itself into your conduct as God accurately reproduces His character in you." This new you, the new woman, is one that has to daily nurtured for your total wellness.

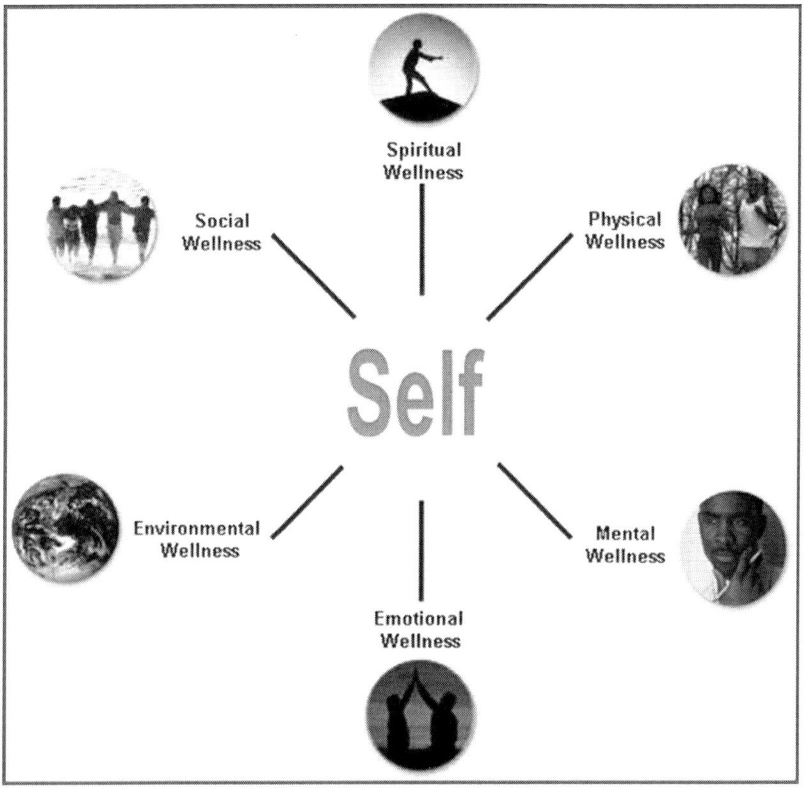

Each of the above areas is a form of wellness that each should assess for their own personal self to locate and decide on a new plan as to how each should be nurtured. Over a period of introspectively looking over my life I noticed how the darkness of my past distracted me from properly nurturing each area of myself that spoke to the total woman of being. However, faith in the process and a renewed attitude made me aware that it is never too late. No matter which phase of life you are currently in, change and reinvention can and will happen. The nurturing wellness of one is a discovery and renewal that can be uncommon to what one is accustomed to in a full awareness of how yesterday only takes and does not give. The past takes away from you, it does not give.

This new woman must give herself permission to properly nurture herself into the place she deserves to be. As the nurturing process begins you will see that your state of being is a choice. The same choice that is made when you decide to stay stuck in yesterday is the same choice you can use to step into the now of today. This is why we make these declarations, we must let our total being know that a new woman, a new person, is in charge. Thus assuring that the nurturing you will give to your spirit, soul, and body will be one that is alarming to your own self and others as well. My father-in-law adamantly spoke to us many times saying, "Growth without change is impossible." This nurturing will require a growth that may seem initially awkward; however, embrace the change that will eventually evoke growth that will be new to all. There is a courage that will elevate, that will grow, out of this nurturing process. Through the Spirit of God all of the wisdom and elements that are needed will be there for you, along with the courage to see it through to your total reinvention. If we need, we must ask. Again, look at the graph and assess what areas you need or desire to nurture within yourself. All you have to do is ask, God said in James 1:5… "If any of you lack wisdom, let him ask God, that giveth to all men liberally, and upbraideth not, and it shall be given him." Through His precious spirit of love for anything you need, He will give. Take a few minutes and ask the Lord two things:

1. What areas need nurturing and wellness in my life?
2. Ask for the wisdom, knowledge and resources that you may need for those areas

Attitude

Attitude of adjustments! Been there and done that! All the things that extenuating circumstances have often brought will leave you with just a downright stinky attitude! Those broken walls, that place of destitute, will leave you in a dark valley of despair that has the ability to affect your total internal awareness to doom and gloom, disgust and hatefulness. The wise old age of proverbs states, "hatred stirs up quarrels," and, "hiding hatred makes you a liar." This venomous attitude has no place in the new you. As stated previously, this is why it is essential that you are committed to your path and journey. There is a continuous discovery that will lead you into maintenance of nurturing your wellness. We have been given the power to change but that daily act and decision has to be made. Alongside it is the proper alignment of the attitude adjustment. I vehemently remember a weekend that I was at a retreat with woman of all kinds from all over. It was as if I had audibly heard the words from God Himself say, "I am fearfully and wonderfully made; marvelous are your works, and that my soul knows very well." (Psalm 139:14) In that moment it was as if the weight of the world had been lifted off of my shoulders and my steps in life became lighter and I seemingly became more pleasant. More pleasant to myself, to my husband, family and others. There was a major attitude adjustment, there was the realization that I did not have to be mad anymore, that I had no more need for co-dependent validations. In that moment, to be perfectly honest, I realized that it is all good. Life is good and things just simply became good. The same can happen for you in a moment. A glimpse from our Divine Creator will adjust your attitude and perspective of life within a matter of seconds and things will completely turn around. It has been witnessed first hand as a total reinvention. For example, going back to school at any age. If you desire to go back to school, adjust your attitude and know that any time is better than no time. Go Now! If you have a desire to lose weight, adjust your attitude and know that it can be done. No longer see the old you. Adjust and see the new you. Do it now! If you have the desire to get out of debt, adjust your attitude and know that you can harness the discipline to get yourself to a place where you owe nothing to anyone! Whatever your desire or dream should be, you must know that this new woman has all the tools to take her reinvention all the way through to the end. However, it is important that you surround yourself with the right relationships and place yourself in a healthy environment that will support and nurture the new woman that you have become. It is important that you are aware of this and that you know that you no longer have to settle for less in your life. You are no longer holding yourself back so there is no need to be around individuals or in an environment that stunt or hinder your growth. Those people, those loved ones from the past, who have grown accustomed to the old you may be surprised with the change and the decisions of change that you've made. These matters, these people and these environments have left you exhausted and have numbed you long enough. Guilt, shame and blame have forcefully antagonized you into believing that you must stay in that place of yesterday this refers to any person, place or thing that you may notice taking a toll on your attitude or re-adjusting your attitude back to that 'stanky gal' place. It is essential that you quickly remove yourself from those people or environments that return you to your old habits.

This is a great time to reposition yourself and undergo a total makeover, a total over haul of yourself. This is a referral to throwing off all the old thoughts, habits, people and environments that have kept you from your new and profound self. Repositioning yourself is an opportunity to really sit back and create an atmosphere of joy and happiness. By the wisdom of God you must select those with whom you desire to share your environment, those who will assist in your nurturing wellness, and who will assist you in the recreation of your new world. Savages and leeches from your past will creep through the crevices of your mind and into your emotions in an attempt to lure you back into your old life. I have witnessed many women who have gone through the total process of change who deceptively tell themselves that they can return to those people or those places or things and supposedly maintain their new lease on life. Slowly but surely, those viscous remnants of the past brought them back to their old, destructive state. So women, give yourself full permission to be the total new woman that you are. You will have to put in the work for your new discovery, the nurturing of your wellness, and the need for an attitude adjustment to maintain the new and improved you. Keeping and maintaining the right attitude will give you the power to live life to its fullest and to do it with no regrets. An attitude adjustment will empower and enable you to properly nurture yourself in preparation for the change you desire. A change in attitude will also spark the courage and confidence that you will need to holistically maintain the new person that you have become. People's actions and their old environments will continue to react or respond to the old you. This is a time for you to discipline yourself through your discovery and journey,. You must have an internal resolve that no one, nothing and no environment will be able to put you into a place of hurt or offense again. This discipline and commitment will continually propel you into change. It will nurture you with the basic essentials that will give you the ability and encouragement to reinvent yourself at any age. It can be done! It all lies within your power of choice and your commitment to the long haul of change. Know this: If you choose you can be and can continue to be fabulous at any age!

Throughout your journey remember your DNA and just be! Be the great woman that you are and were created to be. There is a reinvention awaiting you and only you at this stage can be your own enemy. You are the CEO of your life and you can determine your start and finish. Make a decision today to give yourself a smile and a hug and begin your journey to a new and improved you.

Listed below are some daily principles that will assist you in your journey.

1. Awake daily with determination. Affirm yourself by saying, "Today I choose to be happy." Our happiness is a choice, not a destination!

2. Create your own journal. This is a compilation of your thoughts and ideas so be honest with yourself and say what you want to say. Confront the emotions that you desire to confront. Just relieve yourself of the toxicity and embrace the new beautiful emotion of letting go. Journal your journey.

3. Spend time with yourself, family and friends. Again, remember to surround yourself with people who embrace your new change and who will support you in your reinvention.

4. Find a church, support group or any kind of meaningful organization that will speak to, educate, and cultivate the new you.

5. Exercise and learn healthy habits and seek to destroy bad habits.

Please take time to concentrate on and pray for all of the items listed above. In this time of reflection and prayer, make the necessary decisions and adjustments as God shows them to you.

Reflections and Prayer

Close your eyes and get into a quiet, relaxed place where you can be still and receive God's word. In your heart and in your mind lock onto the new woman that you are and only see this woman moving up from here.

Prayer:

Dear God, please help me in this new place. I do believe that you have given me everything that I need in this life. No more obstacles or boundaries are there. Help and assist me to receive my new change. I ask you to help me to embrace my new change, I ask you to place all around me that which will exemplify your glory. Those things that once brought pain to my life, you have removed and now you will get total glory from the new and ever-evolving life that I will lead, not only for myself but for the help and service of others as well. In deep gratitude I thank you for what you have done now and what you will forever do. Amen

Additional References

Jeremiah 30:1, 7	Psalms 147:3
Psalms 119:165	Proverbs 23:7
Psalms 139:13-14	Philippians 2:5

Notes:

ABOUT THE AUTHOR

Starr Benjamin

Starr Benjamin has invested much of her career in the area of behavioral health. She has worked as a registered nurse in hospital, clinic and health services settings and has also been involved in faith community nursing and in the development of a hospital-based consumer health resource center.

As she embraced her calling to support individuals within a whole person framework and encourage them in their pursuit of optimal well-being, Starr completed her Master of Arts degree in Human Development at Saint Mary's University of Minnesota. She was encouraged by her MA program advisor to explore the area of creative non-fiction writing and was inspired by her Developmental Psychology professor to focus her energy on supporting women through the mid-life journey.

Starr has earned Intrinsic Coach certification through Totally Coached, Inc., completed training in Circle of Life Health and Wellness Coach Training through Health Action, Inc., Wellness Recovery Action Plan (WRAP) facilitator training through the Copeland Center for Wellness and Recovery as well as completed Women: A Journey to Wellness Certification training through PWN.

Writing on the topic of change seemed fitting since Starr and her husband recently relocated to Clear Lake, Iowa after spending the majority of their 28 years of marriage in the St. Paul, Minnesota area. She feels blessed to live near her parents and treasures the time they spend together. Starr and her husband are actively engaged in cheering on their daughter and son as they each transition through college and into their careers and adulthood.

Contact:
Starr Benjamin
Phone: 641-355-3801
Email: sb_benja@yahoo.com

THREE

When Life is Upside Down: Thriving from the Inside Out

By Starr Benjamin

Company layoffs…the empty nest…relocation…financial or health challenges…sometimes a single experience or series of events can cause one to feel as if life is turning upside down! Whether planned or unexpected, for many women, transitions may incite a flood of emotions. The way we confront these events will determine if we merely tread water to stay afloat or if we begin to thrive and ride the waves of positive change.

Much of what I have learned so far about this topic is the result of some challenging times, particularly at the onset of midlife. For many of us, this can be a stage of intense introspection and questioning of life's goals and purpose. I have to admit, there were moments that I did not cope well at all. Throughout this process I began to discover some steps that may help tip the scales from surviving to thriving. The acronym **CHANGE** highlights some of the important qualities necessary to optimally manage these upside-down times.

Be Curious – Learn to develop an inquisitive attitude. A good way to do this is to observe children interacting with their world. My daughter, Nora, was very tactile as a child. This is how she discovered new information. One morning when she was just a toddler, I was occupied with household chores while Nora was noisily played with pots and pans in the kitchen. Soon it became a bit too quiet. That was always a red flag that something was not quite right. I peeked around the corner at her and all I could do was laugh. My little girl was thoroughly engaging her curiosity as she sat on the floor sifting her hands through an enormous mound of flour, instant oatmeal and dry beans among other ingredients that she was now tall enough to reach on the pantry shelf.

How does this story translate to the adult life? Mix things up a bit – figuratively. Entertain possibilities, explore options and seek to learn something new. Be curious. Ask yourself questions like: What would I choose to study if I returned to school? How would I go about changing my career or even transforming my role with my current employer? Who would I like to spend time with if my friends were not available? Are there things I can change so that I might live more healthfully? What hobbies do other people enjoy that I may want to try? Your "pantry shelf" of life is loaded with all kinds of possible ingredients!

It may help to diagram your thoughts as you explore life with a curious mindset while contemplating possible changes. Fill in the oval below to reflect a change you are facing or have been thinking about making. Then fill in the squares after considering: What are my sources for information, for example books or websites? Are there organizations I can connect with or support networks I can join that will help me through this transition? Who are the people that can give me insight regarding which steps to take?

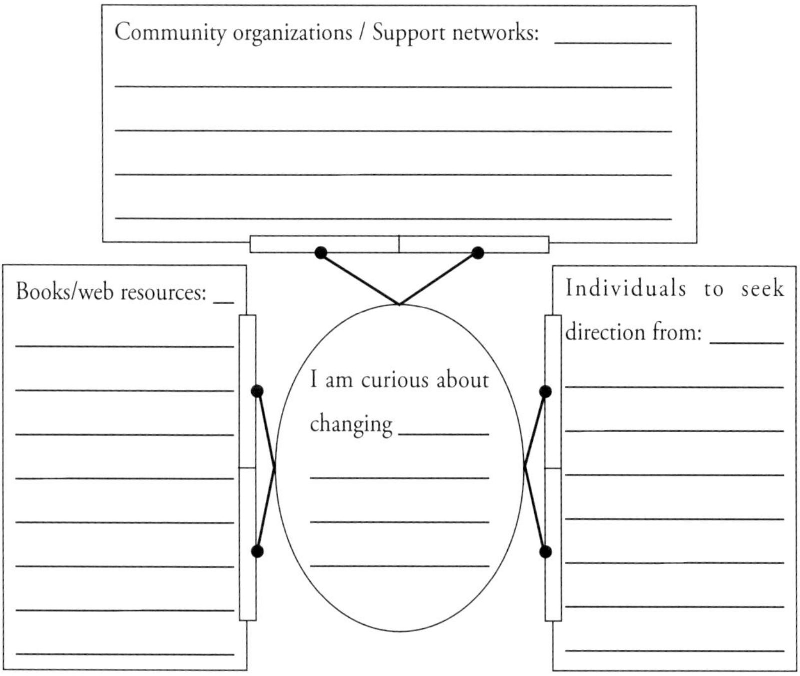

Be Hopeful – Live with a sense of expectancy that positive experiences are right around the corner. This can be very difficult especially if you have encountered a number of life challenges and disappointments. You may find yourself waiting for the other shoe to drop. The automatic "now what?" response pops into your mind and it seems that the more you focus on those negative occurrences, the more ingrained this thinking becomes. This isn't to say that you should permanently don your rose-colored glasses and pretend that there are no difficulties, however. There will always be bumps in life's journey.

Have you ever noticed that there are people in this world who naturally exude optimism? Their hope is contagious. My friend Janis is this type of person. We have journeyed together through some stressful times. I recall an occasion about ten years ago when we sat across from each other on my living room couch. That evening she offered her support when I truly needed it. She was helping me by taking notes as I rattled off information and phone numbers pertaining to the situation that was troubling me. We ended our time together with prayer. After Janis left that evening I picked up the paper with the notes she had written and I noticed that in the margin she had fancily doodled a simple phrase:

There is HOPE!

I tore this message from the larger sheet of paper and taped it to my kitchen cupboard door where it served as a daily reminder. This simple promise anchored my emotions during the weeks to follow. To this day, I have that small scrap of paper tucked away in one of my journals.

Who are the hope-filled people in *your* life?

1. ______________________________

2. ______________________________

3. ______________________________

Surround yourself with these people. Even one person that shares hope is a treasure!

Be Adaptable – The analogy in the Bible of the potter and the clay clearly illustrates this idea of being adaptable or moldable. If you have ever watched a potter work with clay you will notice the precision of his hands as he molds and shapes a nondescript mound of clay into a lovely functional vessel. The clay, in constant rotation on the potter's wheel, undergoes an amazing metamorphosis at the hands of its maker. Isaiah 64:8 beautifully states, "Yet you, Lord, are our Father. We are the clay, you are the potter; we are all the work of your hand." (NIV)[1]

In my conversations with other women I have discovered that I am not alone in my tendency to try and control every last detail of my life. For many years I held onto my own plans with a tightly clenched fist. As my children reached their pre-teen years it became increasingly clear to me that the control I thought I had was only an illusion. It was then that I began to discover that when my fists are tightly clenched they cannot be open to receive the plans God has in store for me.

Journal Your Thoughts: *Are there areas of your own life that you are clenching tightly and not allowing to be shaped and molded?*

____

____

____

____

____

Be Nourished – Paying attention to your physical needs like exercise, sleep and good nutrition, while simultaneously avoiding habits that can be detrimental to your health and well-being, are important to help you towards the goal of thriving from the inside out. Self-care often becomes a low priority when attention is focused on an upside down life. Remember to consult with your health care provider regarding any health recommendations or preventive screening tests you may need. You may also want to consider talking with a counselor or therapist to help you with the emotions that accompany transition.

In addition to nourishing the body we must also feed the mind. Be a lifelong learner and challenge your brain to process new information. This goes back to cultivating your sense of curiosity. Read books on a broad range of topics. Listen to the stories of the people you meet and recognize the value each individual brings to your life.

Most importantly, nourish the spirit by reading God's Word, spending time in prayer and worshipping together with others. I find that getting out into nature and viewing God's creations deeply nourishes my spirit. On a recent winter morning in Iowa I opened my drapes to an incredible panorama of frost-laden trees and tiny glistening ice crystals that seemed suspended in mid-air as they reflected the morning sun. When I stepped outside I felt surrounded by the Maker's handiwork and my spirit soared. Feeding your spirit may occur in such simple ways when you take the time to open your eyes and experience the creation that surrounds you.

Write down key words to identify your goals for nourishing:

Body ______________________________________

____

____

____

____

Mind ____

____

____

____

____

Spirit ____

____

____

____

____

Be Grateful – Dr. Robert Emmons, Ph.D. is a professor and leading expert in positive psychology. He has directed scientific research on the practice of gratitude and highlights some of these studies on the following academic website - http://psychology.ucdavis.edu/labs/emmons. The research has found that, "grateful people report higher levels of positive emotions, life satisfaction, vitality and optimism and lower levels of depression and stress."[2]

Many have promoted the idea of keeping a gratitude journal. This can be a powerful practice especially when you are going through periods of transition. At a time when an individual is vulnerable to negative thinking, searching for the blessings amid the trials can result in a refreshing shift toward positivity.

Listing what you are thankful for is not a novel idea. I recall the chorus and one of the verses of an old hymn that my Grandmother loved:

Are you ever burdened with a load of care? Does the cross seem heavy you are called to bear? Count your many blessings, every doubt will fly, And you will keep singing as the days go by.

Refrain:

Count your blessings, name them one by one, Count your blessings, see what God hath done! Count your blessings, name them one by one, And it will surprise you what the Lord hath done.[3]

Yes, even when this song was written in 1897, before the research was available to back the theory people recognized that a grateful heart has the power to lift one's spirit. I would like to challenge you to count ten blessings you can think of right now and write them down on this list.

1. ______________________________

2. ______________________________

3. ______________________________

4. ______________________________

5. ______________________________

6. ______________________________

7. ______________________________

8. ______________________________

9. ______________________________

10. ______________________________

Did you notice any change in your emotions as you completed your list?

Be Enthusiastic – This final quality for optimal transition builds on the previous qualities. You may be saying, "I am afraid. I didn't ask for this change. I am not sure how this is all going to turn out. How can I possibly be enthusiastic?" It would seem natural to conclude that enthusiasm is the resulting response to good outcomes and would rarely accompany the emotionally demanding steps of change. However, the late Dr. Norman Vincent Peale, minister and author of *The Power of Positive Thinking,* positioned the emotion in front of the outcome when he declared, "Life's blows cannot break a person whose spirit is warmed at the fire of enthusiasm."[4]

When we sold our house to move to another state two hours away we had to say good-bye to our wonderful neighbors, the familiarity of our city and the place we had called home for over 24 years. Even though there were many positive aspects to our move, we were often less than enthusiastic during the process and we shed a few tears, especially when making the final tour of the empty shell. Along with taking some time to grieve the home we were leaving we attempted to build enthusiasm by exploring information on our new community and planning remodeling projects for the home we had signed a purchase agreement on. My husband and I also created a list of all of the benefits that the move would offer which we recited to each other when our confidence wavered. Many times we had to act as if we were enthusiastic and soon the true emotion would follow. Essentially, we had to reframe the picture of our future and focus on the positives in the new portrait.

Think of your situation. How can you reframe your picture and paint the positives? What are the elements on which you can focus your enthusiasm? Be creative in the space on the next page.

Living with enthusiasm does not mean ignoring your feelings. Embracing change with unbridled zeal is not always possible. You may need to allow yourself time to grieve the loss of dreams or adjust to the newness of the territory and then work up to a renewed interest in the transitional life you are now living.

Positive change starts with being **C**urious, finding that spark of **H**ope, developing an **A**daptable approach, **N**ourishing body, mind and spirit, practicing **G**ratitude and finally…the **E**nthusiasm builds.

Even when life seems upside down, having these qualities may help you optimally face change that comes your way as you begin to thrive from the inside out.

Notes

1. **THE HOLY BIBLE, NEW INTERNATIONAL VERSION®, NIV® Copyright © 1973, 1978, 1984, 2011 by Biblica, Inc.™ Used by permission. All rights reserved worldwide.**

2. Emmons, R. (2010) Measuring the Grateful Disposition. Retrieved from http://psychology.ucdavis.edu/Labs/emmons/PWT/index.cfm?Section=5.

3. Count your Blessings, *Words:* Johnson Oatman, Jr., Arranged by Excell, Edwin in *Songs for Young People*, by Edwin Excell (Chicago, Illinois: 1897). Retrieved from http://www.cyberhymnal.org/htm/c/o/countyou.htm/.

4. Peale, N. Quotation retrieved from http://quotations.about.com/cs/inspirationquotes/a/Enthusiasm1.htm.

ABOUT THE AUTHOR

ELIZABETH C. PAGÊ

Unconventional approaches and elegant innovation are Elizabeth's passions. She is an early adopter and thrives on complex challenges, decoding myths, and unfolding truths lost to the mists of time personally, professionally, or globally. Elizabeth empowers people with purpose to transform and create a world renewed, inspired, and worthy of you. By mapping your hidden desire and dreams to unconventional wisdom and 21C business training, technology & coaching practices, Elizabeth shines a light on the shadows of half truths disclosing the deception of what can't-be-done and maps a route of how it can.

Elizabeth C. Pagê's raison dêtre is: "creating communities of economic independence for women world wide. *TM She's invented an entrepreneur's road map accelerating emergent economic empowerment by amplifying women's values and impact for global economic transformation through business education, leadership and exchange. WEBX2020 is a 21 C. global membership platform for women entrepreneurs, executives, business leaders and the avant-guard. Enabling and educating ethical entrepreneurs with Web 2.0 and mobile technology is simply the most powerful path to economic independence, equity, and innovation. Coaching and peer to peer learning is the platform for accelerated growth and leadership. Our vision is economic and social transformation.

Elizabeth Pagê is an international development & systems specialist with a focus on coaching women business owner's entrepreneurs and experts and is based in Washington, D.C. and France. She holds a graduate degree in Systems Engineering in Knowledge & Learning (K&L), speaks French & English, and has over two decades designing, collaborating, implementing & managing innovative and award-winning products and services. She worked nine years at the World Bank–an international development bank–where she received the Bank President's Innovation Award for entrepreneurial innovations in K&L.

Eco–Decision Elizabeth was founder and Editor-in-Chief of this international bilingual journal on sustainable environment and economics subscribed in over 100 countries. She also developed and delivered distance education to indigenous peoples in the far north followed by designing and delivering executive education at the prestigious Banff School of Management. Her initial foray into international development was in India followed by successful entrepreneurship serving businesses for 10 years. Her current fun is GPS tracking of her globe-trotting sons and husband.

Call or email today for your complementary coaching consultation.

Contact:
Telephone: 301.312.6606
Elizabeth@webx2020.com

FOUR

A Woman's Vision, Voice and Values

By Elizabeth C. Pagê

Who would you be if you could be anyone? What would you do with your life if you were free of constraints? Where would you be, who would you be with and how would you spend your time? If you discovered that some facts were fiction, would the truth set you free?

You've heard these questions before but what if I could show you a powerful way to find the answers? Here are some ideas about the world that could change the way you see yourself and help you to discover your authentic voice.

Take William Shakespeare for example. If the playwright had been a woman would it open your mind? What if the spear-shaking goddess of the theatre, Pallas Athena, was, in fact, the witty pen name of the noble Elizabethan woman who ruled the page, (mightier than crown and sword) shaping centuries of culture and intellect from a feminine mind?

What about art history's assumptions? Spears become weaver's shuttles when France's cave paintings at Lascaux are interpreted without a bias for dominance, hunting and war, and instead are seen as a celebration of the civilizing forces of domesticity such as harvest, husbandry and the arts.

Women were weavers, artists and inventors and the cave is our hearth. Since necessity is the mother of invention and technology follows function, its logical that cooking and clothing were also women's inventions. Consider the sensuous shape of an amphora pregnant with stored grain and wine. The cave's cartoons of horned bulls resembles the shape of a woman's womb and ovaries. Perhaps an homage to fertility goddesses?

And today? There is contemporary evidence of women's power hiding in plain site. The fact that women represent a greater economic force than the combined economies of China and India makes us a mighty market. The fact that a majority of university graduates and business start-up CEOs are women belays the reality that board rooms and political offices hold few female decision makers. If women were counted among the most powerful, wealthy and talented leaders in the world, would our voices be heard? If your voice was heard, what would you say?

Taking this critical step toward finding our voice is a small step from exile to empowerment—from the fragmented and displaced to an integrated framework—a tapestry on the loom. On this framework we weave new visions for our lives and perhaps for the world. What threads of history can we follow to a skein from which an authentic history of women's wisdom and power is woven?

While following that thread of history we find that women lost their way through trauma and time. However, we also discover that domination is sustained, in part, by our complicity in the myth of patriarchy's predominance. It's time for women to claim our voices, amplified in chorus and united in a purpose.

Your story is your power and sharing it releases healing beyond yourself through vision, values and voice and amplified in relationships, partnerships and connectedness. That is the secret revealed. Women are a generative force on earth. Your voice has been masked for too long and it has needed so much. Your voice is too important to forget and too urgent to deny.

I learned that finding my authentic voice was less of a journey and more of a call to action. My call is to empower women to amplify the choir of women's voices world-wide into an undeniable economic force. I chose entrepreneurship because of its leadership leverage. The elegance of entrepreneurship is that it has no gender. We neither ask for permission nor apologize for our enterprise.

Entrepreneurship is a generative model that forms, informs and transforms the domination model. Entrepreneurship is a dynamic system that mimics the generative state of women and regenerates in us our capacity to become what we once were in the world—powerful creators.

Entrepreneurship is an expression of our unique leadership. As we set conditions to accomplish our purpose we generate, create and inspire transformation in others. The power to transform is a choice. Transformation occurs at that moment when we find and use our voice. In finding that authentic voice we effect transformation not only in our lives, but we transform the lives of those we reach.

But beware. A calling is not easy and neither is entrepreneurship. I'm reminded that raising our voice is dangerous and history is littered with the bones of crusades for hunted heretics. "Our deepest fear is not that we are inadequate, but that we are powerful beyond measure."

(Attributed to Nelson Mandela) I own that fear. I am guilty of playing roles rather than being authentic, of subverting dreams and passion in pursuit of career, success and legitimacy while attempting to balance family and integrity.

Some women are born brave souls knowing themselves and raising their voices despite their fears. I was not one of these women. Trying to find my voice at this stage of my life is a frightening endeavor because it demands facing myself. Loud noises make me tremble. Numbing my feelings, hiding my fears and forgetting were the keys to my success. I laughed recently when my sister, reminding me of our childhood, informed me that Alzheimer's would be my friend and restore my memory.

Pain is a powerful force for success but it is also deeply disorienting. Sustaining a lifetime of secret shame due to abuse energized and exhausted me. Incapable of trusting myself and others, I compensated with enough innovation to earn considerable success. However, my fears robbed me of my voice, so instead I developed competencies to wards-off challenges.

I was successful though drained from my international career and stressed out as a working mom and wife. I began my life's work in India and became an entrepreneur for the freedom and challenges it provided. Success lead to an award-winning international career over an arch of 20 plus years but my creating, generative soul suffered in the bureaucratic labyrinth. The more senior I became, my capacity to serve became weaker. I attempted to reconcile my passion and youthful promise to serve the poor with the privileged life I created.

I arrived at a crossroads. Would I lock into the pension path or take a stand for my passion? I was so afraid of failing. I hated the thought of looking foolish to my colleagues. I felt I had so much to lose. But in fact, I had something more important to gain—my voice.

Starting a business based on my vision for global economic opportunity and equality wasn't about making a fortune or proving myself all over again. It was a time to reveal myself and to go for my dream of creating communities of economic independence for women world wide" (TM) via entrepreneur education.

But, life is complicated. My husband's prior heart attack was disorienting. Our teenager went from charismatic to a youth at risk. Our second son shouldered much of the confusion on his own. I was facing the fact that my mother was dying. Weeks by her bedside were comforting but the proverbial slap-in-the-face came within hours of her death. I was punched to the floor shattering my dream-like hope for family reconciliation. Eventually restoration came in a most unexpected form—learning to deal with PTSD or, post-traumatic stress disorder bringing order to patterns of chaos in my life. The following exercise was transformational moving from powerless to empowered. By sharing these steps you too can recover your life's purpose by discovering your vision, voice, and values... too important to forget and too urgent to deny.

It is our responsibility to be the voice of the voiceless--that feminine echo that remained silent through the millennia--to express the narrative that in the beginning, created the world, and today wants to create the future by simply sharing our story.

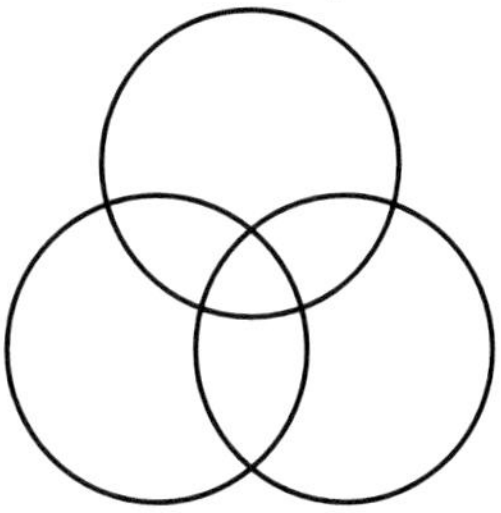

At our core is our generative, relational nature linking our vision, amplified by action through our voice and empowered by our values. Three interlocking circles create a deep inner connection and by its position and function, at the center, is the matrix—womb—where women exercise creative power, purpose and vision preserved deep in the hearth carved on the walls of ancient caves and in stone figurines of swollen-bellied goddesses.

Take a few minutes to work through this exercise. The challenge is to discover the deeper purpose of our lives and to use these three simple steps to discovering our Vision, Values, and Voice.

Let's begin with these steps:

1) A mental journey—clarify your purpose;

2) Mapping your journey—relationships and collaboration;

3) Committing to action—creating;

4) Activate your transformation in only 15 minutes a day over the next 30 days.

Preparation:

To derive the greatest value this process is best done as an interactive group activity but I've adapted it for your immediate benefit so you can do it now. Ideally, find a partner or team to do this with. If you would like me to personally guide you on this journey, contact me by email at: Elizabeth@www.webx2020.com for a complementary guided session. If you would like to receive a list of 30 values to help you in the exercise, email me and I'll send it to you personally.

Begin by assembling colored pens or pencils and a large sheet of paper.

Draw three interlinked circles where all three intersect in the center.

These three parts signify:

1. Your big picture--Vision
2. Your relationships—Voice
3. You the individual—Values

Step 1: Discovering your Vision

Take a journey to discover your Vision and reveal your authentic voice.

First, read through this paragraph of instructions and then find a comfortable position, close your eyes and relax.

... Take several deep breaths and release all of your concerns and thoughts.

... Count down from ten down to one slowly while each breath releases tension from your mind and body.

... Form a mental picture of a beautiful, safe and inspired place. Be attentive. Hear the sounds, feel the sensations and bathe in the colors, smells, and sensations of peace, beauty and creation.

... You are travelling to the outer limits of the universe where there is no space or time.

... Invite someone along on this journey--people known or unknown either famous or familiar.

... Travel into the past or future. Travel to the edge of your imagination and go to as many places as you desire. Change your traveler group or stay with the original ones. Do extraordinary things, have unbridled conversations, have fun and meander to the far reaches of your mind. Continue until you are fully satisfied.

... Now, begin your return home and bid goodbye to your companions. You're back in your room, seated in your chair. Gently, safely, comfortably, contentedly and completely fulfilled, open your eyes.

This could be five minutes or 15 but to be more relaxed set your phone alarm to signal your return so you don't drift off to sleep. When you hear the timer, remember that its the universe signaling your homecoming.

Welcome back.

Step 2: Finding Your Voice

1. The universe or the big picture. Take a few moments to draw pictures and symbols in the first circle depicting the places you visited. Record your thoughts, feelings, insights and sounds.
2. The second circle is for your relationships: write the names of your travelers to remind you of their wise counsel and draw pictures to capture the new ideas they inspired. Leave space for later.
3. The third circle is for your values: record your deepest insights, feelings and inspirations you experienced on the journey.

Step 3: Empowered by Values

Create and clarify your narrative by sharing your story with a trusted friend or advisor.

1. Go back to the Vision circle, the universal space, and use bullet points to capture the ideal vision of what you would like to create in the world. Use images, symbols or words to express your experience. Don't pre-judge these thoughts and remain open to what comes up. Complete this circle with your bullet points.

2. In the Voice circle, relationships, list the people who would support you in your Vision. Record the names of those who will support you and those who would oppose you. Use +/- signs as indicators. Who are the people in your current reality who would be likely to react positively to the worldview you just captured? Who might react negatively?

3. The third Values circle is you. Situate yourself here. Where do you stand in the world you just created on your journey? Your values tell you volumes about what you will and won't do and in what order of importance. If, for example, it's family, income, education, justice or equality, your choices will be determined by the hierarchy of values—which ones you place above the others. This will determine how you live out your vision and place yourself in your community of support and place of action.

4. In the inner core, the heart of the intersecting circles, now consider all the elements from your Vision, Voice and Values and identify the ACTIONS you can take or ways you can contribute to the vision over the days and months ahead. These bullets are placed at the heart of the intersecting circles. This is your vision in reality.

An Interpretation of the Three Circles

Here is an explanation for a clear understanding of how the three circles relate to your Vision, Voice and Values.

The Vision circle represents that largest field, the gnosis or knowledge. Its that higher purpose, higher power, or higher intelligence in the universe that informs and inspires your life. Its where there are no limits on resources, space or time, making your journey completely free—free from influence and control. It is where your imagination becomes rich and your inner resources have no limits except for those you place on yourself. It is the space of openness and possibility. It resides far from our control but it informs and motivates our actions and relationships throughout our lives. It is the power of purpose—your Vision.

If you appreciate being in this space more than the others then you are a visionary and you are passionate about the big picture and its possibilities. In stressful situations you tend to take the "high" road, see the silver lining in a setback and find opportunities in challenges. Your relationships and actions are coherent and consistent with your purpose once you've identified it.

The second circle—Voice: finding and amplifying your authentic voice through relationships. Here, you create your narrative to share your vision with others which is what connects you to others and builds relationships with them. This is where you gain traction and leverage for your ideas and projects. Aligning yourself with supportive relationships while learning how to leverage or mitigate the countervailing forces is the key amplifying your voice.

If you're energized by this circle you're a person who operates successfully in cooperation and collaboration with others when you are engaged and connected. This is the space in which purpose integrates and intersects with reality and where you create leverage to achieve your higher aspirations. Once clear, this is the point at which other people who share your ideals start showing up in your life, amplifying your voice.

Finally, the third circle—Values: is where you stand alone taking responsibility and action. It is where you are empowered by choosing and ordering your values. It provides the prerequisite structure and systems that make the civilized world turn. In our personal case it is setting the conditions and creating the platform upon which to voice your vision and achieve your purpose. It harmonizes your life, work, family, community and society.

You increase your capacity for making choices when you are aligned with your vision, values and voice. If you have a preference for operating in this space—the inner circle—you prefer concrete actions, projects and results that you can sink your teeth into, put your hands on and control.

Strengthen Your Voice:

Journal for 15 minutes each day for the next 30 days. Activate your Vision, Voice and Values. Each morning reflect on your Vision, amplify your Voice in relation to the people you'll encounter, and given your Values take intentional steps in the direction of your higher purpose. Record your journey, your action steps and the results each day. Send me your questions or insights as you go along. Report your transformation at the end of the 30 days via email to Elizabeth@webx2020.com. We'll share our results and strengthen our voice.

ABOUT THE AUTHOR

Regina Turner

Regina Turner is an accomplished and dedicated professional with over 12 years in the field of education. She is passionate about working with and inspiring both teens and women to achieve the highest vision they have for themselves.

She is in the process of launching The Boswell International Institute, an organization specializing in wellness retreats and workshops for teens and women.

Ms. Turner has a Masters of Science Degree in Biology from North Carolina A&T State University in Greensboro NC and a Bachelors of Science Degree in Biology from Bethune-Cookman University in Daytona Beach, FL

Professional Memberships

Professional Woman Network
Toastmasters International

Certifications

Diversity Trainer with special emphasis in Women's Issues
Licensed Massage Therapist
Biology Teacher

Retreats and Workshop Topics

Spa Retreats
Emotional Wellness for Women
Life Skills for Women
Diversity Training with emphasis on Women's Issues

Contact:
Email: Reginaboswell8865@att.com
Phone number: 954 937-5586

FIVE

Healing The Little Girl Within

By Regina Turner

"God grant me the serenity to accept the things I cannot change, the courage to change the things I can and the wisdom to know the difference."—Reinhold Niebuhr

You cannot heal what you will not acknowledge. It's 2:00 in the morning and I am forced to acknowledge that unworthiness is a core belief that I possess. After being stood up by him yet again, I am left alone to ponder the question of why he continues to reject me. Was I not interesting enough? Could I have loved him differently? What was wrong with me? As countless questions bounced around in my thoughts an even more disturbing question began to emerge in the far recesses of my mind. How could I allow my self-worth to deteriorate to the point of accepting such inconsiderate and thoughtless behavior from him for so long.

Unfortunately, this was not the first time that I'd been left feeling rejected and hurt by a lover's selfish and thoughtless behavior. However, this time I sensed that it would the last. I had grown tired of longing for unavailable men. I was ready for change. The question was how? How do I begin to heal that part of me that felt unworthy of receiving the best that love has to offer? I went to the one place I knew I'd fine that answer - within. Through prayer and meditation I was able to tap into my higher power which I knew to be God. Standing on the biblical principle found in John 16:23: Ask and you shall receive, I asked God to reveal and heal the wounded part of me that had kept me from valuing my worth. The process of going within resulted in a soul searching journey that would take me back in time to my childhood when the erosion of my self-worth began.

My Story

The Beginning

At 15 my heart was completely open to giving and receiving the kind of love that movies were made of. So, quite naturally, when I fell head over heels for one of the most popular boys in school, I expected my affection to be received and returned. For a while he obliged. His smile and winks served as indicators that he was really feeling me. To put it mildly; I was in awe of this boy. Literally, when he walked by me he took my breath with him. A simple "hello" from him made my whole day. I felt so special that someone like him would even notice a quiet, non-assuming girl like me. My confidence level was at an all-time high. That high confidence level, however, would be deflated as I would soon find out that the smiles and the winks only served as teasers to reel me into his web of deception. I would learn that his motives were not pure. As it turned out, his interest in me turned out to be purely physical. His sole objective was to have a piece of me. He never really wanted me. Upon this realization, I felt hurt. To my credit, I valued myself enough to decline his offer for the opportunity to get with such a big man on campus. To his discredit, he never spoke to me again. I was beyond hurt. I was crushed. Needless to say my first experience with opening up my heart to allow love in resulted in me being stung deeply. I moved on ultimately, but I wasn't okay. In fact, I wouldn't be okay for many years to come. At the age of 15 I internalized the belief that I was not adequate enough to "reel in the boy". This internalization would take root in my core belief system and would continue to grow with each failed relationship.

The Middle

From the age of 15 well into adulthood every relationship that I became involved in was a quest to prove to myself that I was good enough. I was never attracted to the nice guy or the available guy. I would set my sights on the popular or high-profile guy. My mission was always to prove that I was adequate enough to "reel in the boy". I'd do whatever it took to win him over. Once my mission was accomplished, I'd move on. I had to fill that insatiable need to feel wanted. Relationships became a game to me. It was such an empowering feeling to be on the winning end. Unfortunately, this was not a fool-proof method of avoiding pain. The problem occurred when the guy that I had targeted couldn't be won over. Because of my need to feel wanted, I would go into a desperate mode, trying to prove my worth. The harder he was to trap, the more I had to have him. When it reached the point of needing to have a target in my life to feel good about myself, I knew I was on the losing end of that relationship. I would find myself lowering my standards and accepting unacceptable behaviors from him. Eventually, the guy would lose interest and move on but not before chipping away another piece of my self-worth. Once again, I'd be left feeling that I just wasn't adequate enough to "reel in the boy". Love, for me, had become a twisted game that would be impossible for me to ever win. If this cycle was to ever end I had to heal that little girl who was constantly trying to be wanted by the boy who rejected her at the age of 15.

The End

So, there I sat, alone at 2:00 in the morning with just me and my thoughts. I was in deep reflection. It had been nearly thirty years of running, ducking and hiding from my emotions. I had been too afraid to feel the hurt that I associated with the act of loving. But now, I had grown weary and had finally reached the point in my life where I wanted to feel love. The last time I opened up myself to it was at the age of 15. The rejection I felt from that experience caused me to close a part of my heart that would ultimately interfere with my ability to feel love. I was ready to open up again. This time was different because the love I craved was not the love of a man, but the unconditional love of God. I desperately wanted that connection to my Father. Without it, I was lost. I simply asked Him to come into my life. It's almost as if God had been patiently waiting on me to invite Him, because as soon as I did ~~that~~, things began to unfold in my life in a way that would propel me to my highest good. I just needed to ask. It is not in His nature to force His will on us. I understood that my healing would only come by surrendering my warped way of loving in the past and give in to God's way. I opened my bible to 1 Corrinthian 13: 4-7 and meditated on the word regarding the bible's expectation of us with regards to love. I meditated on these words daily until they became a part of my spirit. According to 1 Corrinthian, love is patient. It is kind. It does not envy. It is not rude. It is not self-seeking. It is not easily angered. It keeps no record of wrongs. It does not delight in evil but rejoices in the truth. It always protects. It always trusts. It always hopes. When we move away from God's way of loving, we suffer the most.

Steps to Healing the Little Girl Within

Step 1- Acknowledgement

The first step to healing the little girl within was to acknowledge my feelings of unworthiness. Like many people, I wore a mask to disguise those feelings. I was very well put together on the outside but very scattered on the inside.

Step 2 – Asking and Receiving

The universal law of attraction will always work to bring to you what you ask for. If you want to know the answer, ask the question. All answers are found within. You must still your mind to receive them. I asked God to reveal to me the origin of my hurt and He did by allowing me to travel back in time when it occurred. By going back in time, I was able to understand and correct my behaviors.

Step 3 – Establishing a Connection With God

I invited God into my life and asked Him to direct my steps. For years I tried to do it without him. The results of not living a God-centered life had me sitting up at 2:00 in morning feeling rejected and unworthy.

Step 4 – Surrender

The greatness of a man's power is the measure of his surrender – William Booth. Once you have asked God for anything, allow his will to be done. It will always result in your highest good. Let go and let God!

Step 5 – Visualize

Envision what you want to see manifested in your life. Cut out meaningful words and phrases and paste them to a large sheet of construction paper. The cut-out images should be things that you would like to do, be or have. The law of attraction will ensure that these things will be drawn to you. My vision board was a depiction of a healthy romantic relationship. I would see these healthy images each day upon rising and falling to sleep. The images had become ingrained in my subconscious. Within 30 days I attracted and began dating a man who possessed the qualities I sought in a man. We have maintained a beautiful relationship for the past two and a half years. It really works!

The Lesson Learned Through Healing

On my path to healing the little girl within, I realized that everything I have gone through in my life – the hurt, the rejection, the disconnection from God - was all a part of the divine plan to for me to establish a connection to God. Without it, I could never have healed. Upon establishing that connection, I ~~now~~ realized that God is love and because He lives in us, we are love. Love is an inside job. You cannot find it outside of yourself if you have not connected with the love (God) on the inside. Today I am able to love with a God heart, unconditionally and without judgment. If I give love to another it is his business whether he chooses to return it or not. I allow my love to be free-flowing. I have learned that love I've given will always find its way back to me. If God could love us unconditionally with all our faults and shortcomings, demanding nothing in return, then who am I to demand more than God? Because of my new found revelation I no longer attract people in my life out of a need to feel worthy. I know that I am worthy because I am a child of God and God don't make no junk! I have since forgiven the boy who rejected me at the age of 15 because I now know that it was never about him, it was always about me learning to love myself.

Exercise: Steps to Heal Your Little Girl Within

Step 1 - Acknowledge

I, ____Acknowledge that ____ ____ is an area in my life that needs to be healed.

Step 2 – Ask and you shall receive

God, I want to healed of ________________________________ ____ ____________________ What would you have me do to receive my healing? Be still and wait for the answer.

Step 3 – Establish a connection with God.

Describe what your life has been like without relying on God for guidance.

____

____

How different would your life have been had you trusted God to work things out for you? ______________________________

____

____

Step 4 – Surrender

I surrender

____

____

May your will be done. Amen

Step 5 – Visualize

List at least 10 things you want to manifest in your life

1. ______________________________________

2. ______________________________________

3. ______________________________________

4. ______________________________________

5. ______________________________________

6. ______________________________________

7. ________________________________

8. ________________________________

9. ________________________________

10. ________________________________

Find images of these things and cut and paste onto a vision board. View it daily to draw things into your life.

ABOUT THE AUTHOR

CAROL FISHER

Carol Fisher is the President of Fisher Consultants – Image by Design in Las Vegas, Nevada. She has been in the legal field, and is a graduate of USC Law Center.

She has studied fashion design at UNLV, and completed Certificates in Fashion Design and Merchandising, Business and Hotel Management.

Ms. Fisher has also been one of the contributing authors for two books published by the Professional Woman Network Publishing.

Her education and experience also includes having attended UCLA and USC School of International Relations. She was also a scholarship student as well as having been a scholarship student at the American School of Dance-Hollywood, and a featured dancer as a member of Los Angeles Dance Theatre and Dance Players. She has also been a dance instructor for the Gifted Children's Association, of the Los Angeles School District.

Ms. Fisher has also served two sessions as a California State Senate Page, and a State Resolution was passed in honor of her birth.

Carol Fisher is available to present seminars both within the United States and abroad.

Contact:
Carol Fisher
(702-340-0270)
Email: fishercl@cox.net

SIX

After Caretaking: Entering the Next Phase of Your Life

By Carol Fisher

"May there always be work for your hands to do;
May your purse always hold a coin or two;
May the sun always shine on your windowpane;
May a rainbow be certain to follow each rain;
May the hand of a friend always be near you;
My God fill your heart with gladness to cheer you."
—An Irish Blessing

I was my Mother's caretaker for approximately 10 years. The day after she passed I found myself standing in the middle of the living room wondering what to do with myself. It was early December - early evening – very dark and cold outside. Suddenly, there was all this free time that I realized I didn't know how to fill – free time that I had often wished I had. Now that I had it, I didn't know what to do with it.

As I was standing there I suddenly realized that, for the first time in my life, I was completely alone. My brother had died in infancy and my Father had passed away over twenty years ago. I asked myself, "What do I do with myself, now?"

For several months I had felt as though I was in a fog. The following January I decided that I needed to get out of the house and do something with my time. Just sitting around the house wasn't doing me any good and I realized that life was passing me by. Fortunately, I found a part-time job in a bank that was a perfect fit for me. I was around an exceptionally nice group of people, and looked forward to going to work every day. It gave me a reason to get out of bed in the morning although I knew it was only a temporary panacea.

I began looking for information to start some kind of a part-time home based business. Something that would naturally be lucrative but that would also offer some kind of personal fulfillment while occupying all of the free time.

I enrolled in several classes presented by SCORE and made several trips to the library, borrowing books on things like starting home-based businesses, thinking like a millionaire, and women as entrepreneurs etc. During my research I also ran across books on self-improvement. One book that I am currently reading is by Linda Ellis Eastman called, **Starting Over-Learning to Love Yourself**. As I read each chapter I reflect on it and attempt to apply this new-found knowledge to my own life.

There are many self-help books on the market that have been written by individuals who have had self-discoveries as well as others by professional psychiatrists and psychologists who have written on the topic of "loving yourself." I believe that the reader often misinterprets this phrase, women in particular. "Loving yourself" can and often does come across as being narcissistic. Rather than being narcissistic it's an opportunity, a chance to realize your true self. It's now the time to be introspective, to see what kind of person you really are and to appreciate yourself as a complete human being - a woman of quality.

Rather than self-love, it is more of an acceptance and an appreciation of your own personal worth. It is now the time to acknowledge your strengths and weaknesses and embrace them. Remember, ***nobody is perfect***. Our positive and negative qualities are what make us human beings and our negatives can be turned into positives which can also be a charming part of our personalities.

Acknowledge to yourself the following:

1. Your talents and abilities
2. Your heart
3. Your accomplishments
4. Your family
5. Your friendships
6. Your educational accomplishments

7. Your career successes

8. Your kindness and generosity

9. How you live your life: ethically and with integrity on a daily basis

10. Spirituality.

This means taking time out of your busy schedule for ***you.*** I read a quote from an unnamed actress a number of years ago. She said, "I spend an hour on myself in the morning so that I can spend the rest of the day on everyone else." What a terrific idea!

When you're a caretaker the care of the person or persons you're caring for takes precedence over everyday life and often you lose yourself in the process. Your hair might not look as good as it could, pulled back in a ponytail for convenience or twisted into something not exactly considered an attractive coif (with numerous revealing hair pins). Your nails…well, when was your last manicure – can you even remember? Application of makeup is little or none as you rationalize that, "no one is going to see me anyway." Your work clothes tend to be sweats, jeans and the ever fashionable T-shirt. Clothes become what you wear to get the work done. Fashion has gone out of your daily life along with many other things. Your eating habits become a bit on the unhealthy side. You're so busy making sure that your patient is being well cared for and fed properly that you tend to forget about yourself. The local drive-thru saves time when you're out running errands and then racing to return home. Exercise is often no longer a part of your life as you're just too tired to even consider squeezing it into your daily schedule. When you're a caretaker to your own family it becomes a

24/7 job. Sitting down to watch the news or a movie becomes a real pleasure – almost a guilty one.

Life for you changes dramatically. When you're caring for an elderly person you are given the responsibility for, not only their daily care (which also includes all illnesses that they may be afflicted with, not just old age), but also for making sure that all doctors' appointments are made and kept. The caretaker is also in charge of all the cooking and laundry, as well as the marketing and maintenance of the home, inside as well as out. Oh, and don't forget that the bills that have to be paid. You become a full-time nurse as well as a full-time home manager. I also want to acknowledge the women that are in the "sandwich generation." They're the ones caring for children as well as elderly parents. My heart goes out to you, and I have nothing but admiration for each and every one of you.

Talents and Abilities

Now is the time for reflection. What am I good at? What do I like to do for fun? What do I enjoy doing as hobbies? Now is the time to take advantage of your free time and start enjoying your talents and abilities. Do you play the piano? Now you can sit down at any time and play for as long as you'd like. Do you play tennis? Go out to the courts and find some people to play a game or two. Do you play golf? If not, get out on the course and take some lessons.

Do you have knowledge of certain things that you'd like to pass on to others? Become a volunteer at your local schools, colleges and churches. Also, volunteering on political campaigns can bring you in contact with individuals that can be a good source of networking, particularly if you are interested in getting back into the workforce.

Do you have some knowledge of something that could be turned into a business? Its never too late to start ***anything***! It's too late when they're lowering you six feet down. Get my drift? Hope so.

Family

Now is the time to reach out and strengthen ties with your brothers and sisters, aunts, uncles and cousins. Friendships can be developed, and you might find out that you have much more in common with them besides just being of the same bloodline.

Friendships

Like family, friendships need to be revisited. Call friends that you haven't seen in ages and get together. A lunch out at a nice restaurant can do wonders. You can re-build friendships and develop a social circle that provides you with companionship. You can spend time with them as well as attend functions together.

Educational Accomplishments

Did you complete your B.A.? Do you have a Master's Degree? A Ph.D.? Why not go back to school, part or full time, to complete your undergraduate degree or obtain a higher one. Also, why not enroll in a foreign language course? Learn a new language and meet new people.

Spirituality

I have never been a religious person but over the last twenty years I have developed a kind of spirituality. I have always believed in God and I have always believed in Jesus Christ; however, I have never really felt comfortable going to church. After my Mother passed I found that reading the 23rd Psalm, The Psalm of David, gave me comfort. I did attend church after her death. It was a very nice service, but for me, a very long one.

Meditation has given me an internal peace that I never had before. Just sitting quietly and looking up at the sky makes me appreciate nature as does watching a hummingbird hover while it eats from a feeder. Sitting in my living room and looking out at my neighbor's green trees brings a moment of tranquility. Taking time to stop and become aware of my surroundings brings a quiet peace and sitting down at the dining room table, and saying a simple prayer brings a quiet, peaceful feeling.

In September I turned 60. I realized I'm now entering my senior years and I decided that I'm going to enjoy every minute of those years. I took a good look in the mirror and decided that starting an exercise program was long overdue. Well actually, I looked at myself and exclaimed, "Who's that!" So, I checked through my medical insurance book and discovered that they will pay for exercise classes at selected facilities. I contacted one multicultural center near my home that offers numerous courses which are indeed covered by my insurance. Needless to say, I have enrolled in Pilates core conditioning which I attend several times a week. The classes are challenging but very worth it. I can't tell you how much better I feel since starting these classes. There is also an olympic-sized, heated pool which many people at the center enjoy. For a while I was going to the chiropractor several times a week. Since I started theses classes; however, I haven't required any chiropractic work. I noticed that there are many seniors attending classes. Just because you're retired and/or over 60 years of age doesn't mean that your life stops. What's that cliché? "Life begins at 60," or something around 60.

When I turned 40 I told everyone within hearing distance that it was my birthday. It was an exciting birthday for me as 40 represents leaving your younger years and entering into womanhood. I read a quote by an anonymous Frenchman who said, "When a woman turns 40, she loses the acidity." As I thought about it I began to fully understand what he meant. You've developed a maturity and you've become secure within yourself. Your life experiences and education have molded you and broadened you into a woman of grace. Personally, I wouldn't be 21 again for anything. Been there – done that! I've learned so much over the years and life has offered me so much like my friendships, various careers and travel. I'm happier now than I've been in years. I attend seminars, take computer classes and go to the movies. Things I used to worry about, I now couldn't care less about. **Age is freeing**.

I'm a member of the Baby Boomer Generation. We thought we could change the world, and in many ways we did. Women can now go to restaurants without an escort. We can be married or not. We can have children or not. We can now head corporations and run governments. There is nothing we can't do, so take advantage of all that's out there!

This is one of the best times of our lives. You can enjoy your grandchildren but you don't have the responsibility of raising them. You can stay up late and sleep in. There are clubs you can join where they go hiking and mountain climbing. There are card clubs, travel clubs, you name it and it's out there! You can go for a walk around your neighborhood and not worry about rushing home to get dinner started. You can eat when you feel like it and not because the clock on the wall shows that it's 6:00 p.m. Why not try a new hairstyle or a new hair color? Why not take a trip to a local department store and have the woman at the cosmetics counter redo your makeup? Why not try a new eye shadow, lipstick or lip gloss? You don't have to make a major change, so just take it one step at a time.

I remember watching an interview with Sophia Loren who is one of the world's great beauties, on "The Dick Cavett Show" a number of years ago. She said that the studio had wanted her to have plastic surgery. She said that they told her that nose was too long and that her chin needed changing. She refused. She said that when you put it all together, it worked. Imagine Sophia Loren changing that beautiful face! Remember the cliché, "Beauty is in the eyes of the beholder." Everyone has their own idea of physical beauty.

I watched a show on one of the educational television stations in Los Angeles over ten years ago. This young woman had produced and narrated a video history of her family for her college thesis. She had asked one of her aunts why she had never had plastic surgery and her aunt replied, "I've earned these lines. Each one represents a time in my life." What an eye-opening statement! Plastic surgery is truly wonderful for those born with physical facial deformities, afflicted with disfigurement from auto accidents or severe burns. It can bring happiness to some, but it can also bring disastrous results to others. Surgery is surgery. When you go under the knife complications can happen. I'm not discouraging it because the results can and will open doors, doors that might possibly have been closed previously. Plastic surgery can and does change the way we feel about ourselves and if you get the results that you hope for, well, more power to you. However, be cautious.

Get up every morning with a positive attitude. Get dressed and go out even if its just for a walk around the block. You'd be amazed how much that can make a difference in your day rather than staying in the house day after day. Enjoy your life – every minute of it. If there's something that you're not happy about, change it! Don't wait. Time is ticking away. Don't let anything hold you back. Get up and out and enjoy this phase of your life's journey. Good luck!

Notes:

ABOUT THE AUTHOR

KATRINA EVERHART

Katrina grew up in LA, earned her Bachelor's at Stephens; Masters at University of Missouri, & is ABD at Walden University. Specializing in conflict resolution/mediation, qualitative and quantitative research, systems theory, organizational behavior, project management, competitive intelligence, sea research, and decision sciences she's worked in China, Hong Kong, Malaysia, Vietnam, & the US, training & conducting product research, product/service development & marketing. Past projects include Sprint's DSL, Talking Call Waiting, P&G Floor Care, American Express's Leadership Development. She is an author, Certified Project Manager, Mediator, Professional Researcher, Indexer, Underwater Naturalist/archaeologist, and Parliamentarian. She manages her 180 year-old family cattle farm.

Her avocations include social entrepreneurship, organic farming, drying herbs, making herbal teas, yogurt, cheese, pasta, soap, natural dog biscuits/treats, candles, knits and crochets, and collects individual size personal items such as shampoo/ soap for homeless or women's shelters, and helps with genealogical research for DAC. Presentations include: Parliamentary Procedures for Everyday Organizations, Protecting Yourself from Identity Theft, Family Business Differences, Mark Twain, Missouri Indians, Olive VanBibber Boone, Thomas Paine and Common Sense. She volunteers as a therapeutic clown, scuba dives, and racewalks competitively. She is a Registered Yoga Teacher (RYT) in Hatha & Kundalini yoga and is also certified in Yoga in Chairs for MS, Reiki, Pilates, Tai Chi, Qigong, and Zumba.

Other Memberships:

- American Association for Public Opinion Research.
- American Institute of Parliamentarians.
- American Society of Indexers.
- Association for Consumer Research.
- Association of Conflict Resolution.
- Association of Missouri Mediators
- Association of Qualitative Research Practitioners.
- Association for Applied & Therapeutic Humor
- Clowns of America International
- Heartland Mediators Association.
- International Indoor Air Quality Association
- Mediators Beyond Borders
- National Association of Parliamentarians.
- Professional Woman Network

Contact:
Katrina Everhart
Electronic Surveys and Polling, (or ESP) LLC.
573-234-6222
KatrinaEverhart@yahoo.com

SEVEN

In the Line of Fire: Conflict Resolution at Work

By Katrina Everhart

Attitude determines altitude… as long as we know how to do deal with conflict. Conflict occurs every day with family, friends, co-workers, service personnel and even strangers. Whether reading a Shakespearean play where the antagonists create conflict in the 15th century or watching a reality show like *Undercover Boss* or *The Apprentice* we see conflict based on people's different experiences which form their opinions. Interest and intrigue occur when we read about conflict in a book or see it in a movie or on a television show. It causes difficulty every day and creates stress for individuals who deal with it in the workplace. In the workplace an antagonist is not so funny or interesting. We often think of this as destructive conflict and destructive conflict takes time, decreases productivity and increases stress. Altering words, changing styles and reviewing even the simplest of actions and behaviors can change conflict. Constructive conflict can help us create new processes, procedures, products, services or a combination of all. In many cases, if it were not for constructive conflict resolution we would not have many of the personal items that make our lives easier everyday like electric lights, automatic thermostats and refrigerators which allow us store food.

Personal Experiences and Workplace Conflict

Workplace conflict, in part, deals with both personal and professional perspectives. While some believe the workplace is just an extension of their home with a different family. Others believe that the workplace is **no** place for personal comments and issues and this alone brings conflict into the workplace. Conflict also arises due to different perspectives and experiences. The phrase, "common sense" is repeated frequently in both personal and professional settings.

Common sense is based on experience and education, whether formal or informal. One easy way to recognize the differences comes from car braking. Before anti-lock brakes (or ABS) drivers were taught to pump brakes for traction. With ABS, pumping the brakes causes problems. In fact, some individuals have been killed when ABS engaged and the driver released and pumped. What was common sense for decades is now dangerous and even deadly! Of course, in many situations the differences will not be so stark. We must realize that some folks do see some items as polar opposites rather than different degrees along a continuum. Different experiences, teachings from formal and informal education and beliefs create different personal and professional perspectives, all of which can create conflict. One such example often used in the workplace is the Golden Rule.

Golden Rule

We have all heard the Golden Rule, *Treat others as we treat ourselves and/or family.* This has the same problem as the brakes. Some people grew up in homes where everyone cared for each other and their welfare while others did not. For example, we all hear about how folks who grow up in alcoholic homes are more likely than others to become alcoholics themselves. Those who grow up in ~~an~~ abusive homes are more likely to become abusive; and, those who grow up in impoverished homes are more likely to be in poverty themselves as adults. Certainly, there are many success stories from individuals who have come from alcoholic, abusive or impoverished homes who overcome these issues, but the recidivism rate is still quite high. Think about the unfortunate example recently with Ted Williams, the homeless man made famous for the golden voice. Within 45 days of becoming famous and starting drug and alcohol rehabilitation, he left the facility to go back to the streets.

It takes work to change one's mindset and habits. This we can all agree upon. Change often creates conflict within the individual, personally and often professionally. Think about the folks who start a diet and are sabotaged by friends and family when they lose weight. This is not because they do not want the person to succeed but because they do not know how they will fit in when the individual succeeds. Another great example is the story about ~~a~~ homeless teenager Liz Murray who decided to work every day to change her life and wound up graduating from Harvard. In her book, **Breaking Night**, Murray (2010) notes she had to work hard every day to change her life. She began by completing her high school diploma and dealing with professionals in various settings. These simple acts caused conflict with her family and many folks who knew her. They were treating her as they had always been treated. By treating Liz the way they treated themselves they could not understand her desire to change. Yet the outside public loved the story and a movie was made.

While not everyone has been homeless or graduated from Harvard, we often do not realize that we do treat others the way we treat ourselves. This creates jealousy as well as anger in the workplace. For example, one person may think taking the last bit of coffee and turning off the machine is common sense while another will feel this is inconsiderate because they drink coffee all day. Individuals who grow up in families may have been taught one or the other so either could be appropriate and normal given the time of day. In the morning it might be more of a problem than in the afternoon or just before 5 p.m. when folks are going home.

Individuals who may have had an abusive, alcoholic or impoverished family will not understand why their actions or reactions are causing conflict and when someone states, *Treat others as we treat ourselves and/or family,* they can only comment that they did. They do not understand, based on previous experience(s), why the other person is angry. To wit, their personal habits affect their professional interactions and cause conflict in some cases. Yes, it is hard for many to realize that we all have different home based experiences even if we lived next door to each other, in the same city or even on the same street. Taking this one step further, even one person can have different reactions. Think about how a coat can change a person's perspective about the weather. Those who have warm shoes, socks, coats, gloves and clothes often do not mind wintery weather; however, those who do not have warm items do not like winter weather. Recently I lost the use of my house due to a spring flood. This made me acutely aware that even summer was not enjoyable. While I was able to stay in a hotel after the first few days my daily activities such as eating, exercising and project work changed because I did not have access to a refrigerator or the equipment and resources to be efficient or productive. Stress became notable every minute because I had no house to live in and I did not know when I would be able to get back into my house to determine what items had to be replaced and what items were completely destroyed. I had to guard against arguments because I often would not know where I would be staying that night as the insurance company had not determined, along with the city, whether my house was livable or still condemned. The hotel had required me to pack up and be out of the room before I left for work. It is important to note, as well, that the insurance company would not reimburse me. They would only pay the hotel directly. Working in homeless shelters, transitional housing, soup kitchens and food pantries for almost 15 years as well as preparing personal kits for women who had lost their homes to fires, tornados, floods or who had fled their homes due to abuse, I was familiar with all of the items one needed, i.e. a comb, shampoo, soap, wash cloth, tooth brush, tooth paste, etc. Yet, it was two days before I could even get organized enough to find my wallet so that I could go to a store to buy items that I lost and get a clean pair of clothes.

Why tell this story in an article about conflict at work? Because I still went to work these days. I was confused most days. I did not know where things were and it took longer for me to concentrate and accomplish activities. This is true for anyone who is experiencing a crisis. Now remember, a crisis to one person may not seem like a crisis to another person. While most view losing a home as a problem, we work with people who have different experiences that shape their work lives every day, not just for several months. Folks who sleep eight hours in a bed, walk the dog, exercise and have breakfast and coffee before coming to work with little to no traffic have a completely different mindset from someone who runs a farm and sleeps only six hours because they have to get up to feed animals in the morning and then do farm work after they get home from an office. Both of these folks will have a different mindset from a person who slept in their car and showered at the truck stop for $10 before coming to work. Certainly, we like to believe that we know our coworkers yet recent books about even famous folks like Debbie Reynolds noted that the fabulous lives we thought they had were not so fabulous, especially when they were bankrupt. Why think about different home lives and backgrounds? Because they are what shape our perspectives and opinions regarding how we are to treat others and how we will treat ourselves. It does not mean we are bad, it just means we first need to think more inclusively about lifestyles rather than exclusively when we repeat the phrase, *treat others as ourselves.* In some cases, folks are treating you as they treat themselves and they do not understand why this becomes a problem.

Television

Television has become an equalizer in US society. Television has portrayed rituals on various situation comedies (or Sitcoms) such as taking showers, putting on clean clothes, walking the dog and/or exercising before work, eating breakfast and having juice, coffee, ~~or~~ tea or some combination before going to work. While incredulous to some, this seems like a fantasy to others. While we talk about having dinner at a table, many families do not experience eating together at a table and never have, even 50 years ago. One family's children next door went to a private school. Each child got up and had a complete breakfast while their parents quizzed the children on their homework for 15 minutes and lunches were made. The neighbors on the other side got their kids up 15 minutes before they had to be at school and if they got breakfast, it was because they had freezer pops. The parents did not know whether homework was done or not and lunches were never an option. They ate what they could get from the other students in class. Yet, all three homes were next to each other. All were white with black trim and all had around 2,500 square feet. All three sets of parents also worked for the same company in management, earning salaries within 10% of each other.

Television sitcoms as well as reality shows have demonstrated the differences in people's family lives and habits. For example, while the families on shows like *Roseanne* and *Leave it to Beaver* both ate dinner at a table, the habits of the two matriarchs were different. One yelled at children regularly, the other did not and yet neither hit nor spanked their children. We have seen single fathers on television since the 1950s and 1960s with *Andy Griffith* and the *Courtship of Eddie's Father*, but there were public objections to a single mother who was not a widow on *Murphy Brown*.

While incredulous or not, many families learned that hitting a child in certain ways was considered abuse and not discipline based on an episode of *Roseanne* in the 80s. We also learned that calling people names based on their ethnic background or religion was wrong. Drinking to the point of drunkenness every night is not normal. Yelling and screaming are not appropriate especially when we degrade someone, adult or child, for their efforts or lack thereof. Some even learned that breakfast is not popsicles and dinner is not potato chips and cookies from the convenience store or the gas station. These items accompany the teachings that individuals should bathe regularly, wash their clothes and brush their teeth daily. To the dismay of some, they even learned they were supposed to wear undergarments, sleep on sheets in a bed, and that you could purchase items at regular stores to deal with athlete's foot, upset stomachs, headaches, or skin rashes or the like. The other side of these lessons is that some have taken the displays of life to mean that they should look exactly like the actor or actress and should purchase the exact same items from clothes, to shoes, to couches, and kitchen equipment. While good for advertisers, it is not always good for the individuals at home or in the workplace. Here again, folks often use the common sense term. Yet, when sleeping in a bed seems foreign, a person will not have the same perspective as someone who has slept in a bed all their lives and knows nothing different.

Various groups suggest limiting television viewing. While this is optimal in families where a parent(s) are involved and there are various activities, in other families television may be the only version of appropriate adult behavior if there is a parent who abuses alcohol, drugs or other people. Children and adults learn vicariously by watching actors perform actions, talk and dress. Yes, some take it to extremes, but some learn new things and they change. For example, my parents learned that email was used in business from a television show and that online banking could be done as well. It was not illegal as they had once believed and while they never purchased a computer, when I was home with my computer my father had me on for hours just looking up things for him that he had heard or seen on television or read in the paper. The conflict for us was that he would not type the information in himself even though I had other things to do than just spend six or eight hours looking up things for him.

Unfortunately, we still experience folks calling people names that are considered wrong in public, criticizing a boss to an outside person, organization or group, and using language in public that is inappropriate. Just in the last two years folks in for-profit, non-profit and even government organizations as well as television and radio personalities have made comments about their bosses, called a person a name or made inappropriate comments which they could not retract. For these mistakes most were fined, many were terminated and some faced both as retribution. Granted, these were personal observations, but they were made in a professional, public format which created conflict. This is when we need to think about the overlapping personal issues in professional settings.

Folks who do not separate or differentiate their personal life from their professional life risk more conflict in the workplace. Some expect their bosses to be a parent and tell them how they should act and behave, what education they should obtain and what organizations they should belong to so they can earn regular raises and promotions. Granted, some workplaces are set up for individuals who want to be told how to do things and some managers enjoy doing this. They believe that its their job to tell their employees what they should do. Unfortunately, most workplaces expect that the individual they hire will be professional at all times. Employers expect individuals to have the same type of family life they have or had or some semblance of family as portrayed in *Andy Griffith* or *Leave it to Beaver*. When we do not, and our common sense differs because of our different perspectives and experiences, we can experience conflict. Some of it will be latent conflict, meaning there is always some underlying tension because we perceive an issue is based on an action or behavior and some will be open conflict in which we talk and discuss conflict issues.

Vicarious Learning

Television portrays conflict in the home and in the workplace, whether in old sitcoms such as *Becker*, old movies like *Life with Father* or in current movie series like *Harry Potter*, portraying personal conflict for some and professional conflict for others. Granted, each show or movie has a different perspective, time frame and perception of reality, but so do most employees and individuals we come into contact with at work. Some employees believe that what they read in newspapers is true and what they see on television is real, others do not believe either is completely true. As demonstrated in the 2010 mid-term elections, there are folks who belong to witches' covens and believe in magic and witchcraft while others do not. Some are internally motivated while others are externally motivated. Some cannot imagine telling their life story or even any life events to folks they work with while others cannot imagine a day going by without divulging their personal family interactions from the night before or their deepest personal desires and family problems.

We can see what happens to characters on television, in movies and even in real life through- various media venues when they divulge personal experiences at work. To some it seems that common sense would tell you not to divulge personal information or watch television, but experiences differ. Folks do reveal their different experiences and understandings of how to treat others in the workplace based on their personal expectations. This is not new. It has occurred for centuries .

Avoiding the Subject, Person, or Making Jokes

Unfortunately, many people learned in school that they should walk away or make a joke when a conflict occurs. The problem with this is that these people often create more conflict. While one person will say they are the bigger person, the other will say they know they are wrong and are leaving or joking so they do not have to face being wrong and apologize for it. In the workplace, avoiding problems rarely helps improve the situation and making a joke often makes a situations worse. So, what do we do?

First, we have to think about the words we use. For example, repeating the phrase "Treat others as we treat ourselves," can create conflict. While one person is expecting a change, another is having their behavior reinforced. This is why so many professional organizations and companies spell out their work policies, procedures, ethical codes and even dress items. Using the phrase "common sense," again can increase the likelihood of one person thinking another will change while it reinforces what the other person has done. They believe that they are doing the right thing.

Being Your Own Mediator

Understanding conflict is important. The simplest categories to understand include competitive, collaborative, compromising, accommodation and avoiding. First and foremost, we know that avoiding does not really help any situation and we know that sometimes accommodating and compromising can be good in some cases as long as no one is keeping score. Let's admit that we all sometimes feel that if I gave in last time then it is the other's turn to give in this time and vice versa. Unfortunately, this will not work in professional settings. Often it can lead to one person feeling disadvantaged in the workplace. Collaborative is often the hardest category to approach because we are required to share professional information and perspectives yet it is often how new products, services, processes and procedures are developed. -Companies are able to achieve benefit beyond the normal income and increase profits. Competitive methods can be good at times and can be bad at other times. Think about employees who compete to decrease errors with a product. This is good for the company and its employees overall. Yet think about two employees who compete because of a personal dislike of one another and wind up pitting other employees against each other, lowering productivity.

As we all deal with conflict differently we often first need to know what our own perspectives are. Individuals can take the Conflict Dynamics Profile (or CDP) with a certified person, a Life Styles Inventory (or LSI) online or the Myers Briggs test online for free. The CDP individual will help folks become self-aware and learn how they deal with conflict within their work and professional realms. They will be provided with practical approaches that, when practiced over time, can improve their effectiveness in the workplace. The CDP-360 allows individuals as well as coworkers and managers to take the assessment. This helps individuals understand not only their behaviors but also how their coworkers perceive them within the workplace as well as how their managers perceive them within the workplace in relation to their coworkers.

Individuals can also complete the Myers Briggs exam online. The Myers Briggs breaks items down into 16 different typologies, eight of which indicate people are internally motivated and eight of which describe the externally motivated. As we all have different methods of interaction, knowing how we interact with others can be quite helpful. Also, reading the different typologies can help us see another person's perspective more clearly.

Once we have more understanding and knowledge of ourselves and our perspectives and beliefs, we become aware of others differences and we can lessen conflict almost immediately. Our first goal is to communicate, not judge based on our background and experiences. We never want to try and take the upper hand, so to speak, as that could be considered intimidating and a form of coercion or bullying. Words and colloquialisms can easily be misunderstood. Comments such as "*common sense*" and "*treat others as we treat ourselves,*" can increase conflict because of the different meanings these phrases have to each individual. Even just thinking about our approach to the workplace can help us think about why conflict is occurring.

First, items should not be considered personal, they are professional. Additionally, we need to separate the problem from the person and we must listen when the other side(s) speaks. We cannot plan our response to one comment to prove someone is not _____ (fill in the blank). Having an outline of what we have identified as the main issues at hand, we need to express our viewpoint in clear, concise words with no added tones, inflections or incendiary words. It helps to rehearse in front of a mirror because we will hear and see things we never saw or heard before. We need to be sure our items are based in current and up-to-date professional information and not our perception of what is real based on just our experiences. Our training, no matter how recent or how long we have been in the field, is not important. We must have authoritative information garnered within the last couple of years that has been published in a peer reviewed publication. We really cannot just rely on friends, family, managers or coworkers we recruit to our so-called side. We also cannot rely on what we might hear or read from popular media sources whether that be radio, television, newspapers or the internet. Once we express our comments professionally we must listen and take notes about how other sides (it may not just be one other side), fit into our professional information guidelines. If you were using a chart, circling the facts from each side that everyone agrees on, can help immediately identify the similarities. Once we see the differences on our chart based just on the facts, we can then begin to think about options to resolve the conflict together. The first issue is remembering that all sides want a resolution even if we do not expect to see or talk to those individuals or that organization again. The essential questions become: Are we up-to-date professionally? Do we have all the information we need to make a decision? What is the best way to work together to achieve our professional goals?

Recommended Reading

Center for Conflict Dynamics http://www.conflictdynamics.org/products/conflictdynamics.php

The Art of Waking People Up: Cultivating Awareness and Authenticity at Work by Kenneth Cloke and Joan Goldsmith

The End of Management and the Rise or Organizational Democracy by Kenneth Cloke and Joan Goldsmith

Resolving Conflicts at Work: Eight Strategies for Everyone on the Job by Kenneth Cloke and Joan Goldsmith

Resolving Conflicts at Work: Ten Strategies for Everyone on the Job by Kenneth Cloke and Joan Goldsmith

Intelligence Tests. http://similarminds.com/personality_tests.html

Win at Work!: The Everybody Wins Approach to Conflict Resolution by D. Katz.

How To Reduce Workplace Conflict And Stress: How Leaders And Their Employees Can Protect Their Sanity And Productivity From Tension And Turf Wars by A. Maravelas

A Briggs Myers test: http://www.humanmetrics.com/cgi-win/jtypes2.asp

ABOUT THE AUTHOR

ANISE KEY BROWN

Anise Key Brown brings more than 20 years of professional experience in human development, transformation and community empowerment. She possesses a Bachelor's degree in Sociology and has received two Master Degrees; one from the State University of New York at Albany and the other from Miami University in Oxford, Ohio. She has pursued post-graduate studies at Howard University in Washington, D.C. and has obtained certifications in Management from the American Management Association. She has also studied at the John F. Kennedy School of Government at Harvard University. She is a certified ESOL (English for Speakers of Other Languages) instructor and an Adult Literacy Tutor.She has received certification as a Life Coach from the Empowerment Institute in Rhinebeck, New York.

Mrs. Brown has worked for the Los Angeles Department of Human Services and tenured as an Assistant Professor for a private University in North Carolina. Her most recent experiences include program development work for an international women's organization in Washington, D.C. where she lobbied on Capitol Hill for issues related to the well-being and empowerment of women from a global perspective. She is the founder of ANISE, Inc. (**A**nise **N**ewton **I**nstitute for **S**elf **E**mpowerment) which is an organization designed to help women realize their full potential in life. She currently serves as the Director of a local government agency in Silver Spring, Maryland.

As a civic activist, Mrs. Brown has held memberships and leadership positions in a number of organizations including the local chapter of the NAACP, the League of Women Voters, the National Political Congress of Black Women, the National Association of Female Executives and Women in Public Policy among others.

Considering herself to be a world traveler, Mrs. Brown's most recent ventures include an excursion to the People's Republic of China and a journey to the country of South Africa. Mrs. Brown currently resides in the suburbs of Maryland with her husband of 25 years, who is a local attorney. She is also the mother of two college-aged sons.

Contact:
Anise Key Brown
P.O. Box 524
Brookeville, Maryland 20833
(301) 682-6494
anise1@verizon.net

EIGHT

Life After Retirement

By Anise Key Brown

Wow! I cannot wait to retire! For me, retirement is like graduating from high school and preparing to enter another phase of life. Yes, I enjoyed high school and all my wonderful friends at the time; however, I was extremely excited about going to college and experiencing a whole new world. That's how I feel about retirement. I am entering a new phase of my life and I'm writing a new chapter in the "Book of Anise". We should all have such books as we transition from the world of traditional work into a world that we get the chance to create. For the first half of our lives society dictated which roads we were to travel and prescribed the time frames for adhering to societal norms and expectations. You focused on getting a good education or skill in order to get a good job, marry, have a family and pay the bills. You see, I had started working at the ripe young age of 12 when you needed to have a state worker's permit in order to work based on child labor laws. I came from a big family where I was one of five siblings.

My mother was a single parent and though she provided extremely well for us, I wanted more of the amenities of life. So, I sought to provide those extra amenities for myself by going to work. I worked through high school, college and graduate school. I only took time off from the labor force during maternity leave and then a few months after my sons were born. I enjoyed my career which began as a retail clerk and cashier during those high school years and evolved as a college professor, program manager, director and finally government executive. I got to be creative and in-charge, which were two main criteria for me to be happy in my career. Most importantly, I got the chance to make a difference in people's lives and the community I worked in. As a driven person, I put in the extra hours going beyond the call of duty to excel in my work; however, after a while, the continuing fiscal crisis, budget cuts, the stresses of management, office politics, long days and long commutes took precedent over the joys of a satisfying career. I began to look forward to retirement and eagerly anticipated it. It was time to move on and focus on this great new adventure that I had sacrificed forty plus years to finally enjoy. Oh, the "joy of retirement" became my mantra. To be all that I ever wanted to be, to do all that I ever wanted to do and to fulfill my heart's desires was extremely captivating and exciting. It was time to create, design and envision this transitional moment of freedom called retirement. Call it second adulthood, the second half of life, the third of life or "rewirement" rather than retirement or whatever lexicon suits you. For me, I just knew that the world of traditional work, with all its privileges and challenges, was no longer my cup of tea. It was now time to sip and enjoy the smells, aromas and tastes of a new life. I was more than ready to retire so the planning for this great adventure towards retirement began.

I started attending retirement workshops and seminars pursuing a plan for the next phase. The opportunities for self-transformation during our retirement years are astronomical. I knew I had to prioritize so I began to put things in order in anticipation of all the wonderful and joyous things that I would be doing and for me, age was not going to be a barrier. We've all heard the stories of inspiration and motivation about people in their latter years creating some of the best and most successful years of their lives. Grandma Moses became a world renowned artist in her eighties. Ray Kroc franchised the fast food industry with McDonald's after the age of fifty. Frank Lloyd Wright, the award winning architect, created his masterpiece in his seventies and the late fitness guru Jack Lalanne made fitness famous and took it to another level well into his nineties. With all of society's expectations and "should do's" behind us, now is the time to truly accept the fact that we really have the power to change for the better and reinvent ourselves, especially at this age-the second half of life. So what does it take to reinvent ourselves at this stage of life? What are the things that we most want to do? What are the things that we want to stop doing and how will this new person that we are going to create feel? Who will we be when it is all said and done? These are the questions that I asked myself as I eagerly prepared for this new phase. For me, there were five areas I wanted to concentrate on during these wonderful years-during the second half of life. The first area is **health,** the second is **finances,** the third is **relationships** and the fourth and fifth are the kind of **lifestyle** that we want to enjoy and finally the kind of **legacy** that we want to leave.

Health

During the second half of our lives, our health becomes our number one priority and concern. Without our health we cannot live up to our full potential and realize our everlasting dreams. Therefore, upon entering our retirement years we must diagnose the state of our health and begin to take the necessary measures, both preventive and corrective, to ensure that we are nurturing and maintaining the absolute best mental and physical health that we can experience. During our working years we were too busy taking care of everyone else and the care of ourselves was too often overlooked. We were also younger. As we become older, however, the physical and sometimes mental faculties decline and we can no longer to take good health for granted. Studies show that not all of our health issues can be blamed on heredity and genes. We do have control, to a large extent, of how healthy we want to be in our retirement years based upon our environment and our own habits and it's never too late to get started on improving our health.

When I was working full time, admittedly, I was overweight. Early morning meetings coupled with long commutes did not allow me to eat a healthy breakfast. Evenings and late night meetings often prevented me from having a sensible dinner at a sensible hour and meetings scheduled during the day encouraged a quick fast food drive thru en route to more meetings as a substitute for a healthy lunch. Sixteen hour work days (not including the commute) did not allow-any time for any kind of exercise routine, let alone much else. The inevitable outcome of poor eating habits and nutrition can lead to weight problems and an overall deterioration of a person's physical health. Excessive weight also adds to a number of health problems such as heart disease, hypertension and diabetes. In order to fully and joyfully live the kind of life that I expected to live during my retirement, I could not allow poor health to be a part of the plan.

Therefore, immediately upon retirement, I realized there were no more excuses. I decided that I needed to either get healthy and physically fit or wallow in the den of defeat, desperation and dissatisfaction with the current state of my health. When I questioned my doctors about the best plans for weight loss, they often suggested the more known diets like Weight Watchers, Atkins, South Beach or another derivative thereof. I wanted a specific plan from my doctors that I was not receiving to my satisfaction. I realized this was another excuse and impediment to keep me from moving further so I took matters into my own hands. I started reading about and studying nutrition and then consulted with a registered dietician at our local hospital. I got up off the couch and got to work, the kind of work that leads to better health. I started eating right, eating less and exercising every day. In less than six months I had lost sixty pounds. I was looking better and certainly feeling better. When I scheduled a check-up as a part of my "get healthy" plan, my doctor remarked that I was a totally new person and took me off all of my prescribed medications. I felt great. I am not at my ideal weight yet but I have incorporated this healthy way of living into my new retirement lifestyle. When you get ready to live your best life during your retirement years, you must have the body and mind required to maintain, sustain and proclaim your future dreams and purpose for your life.

Finances

When I started making plans for this new stage in my life, I knew that finances would be a major consideration so that I would not experience the much feared "bag lady syndrome." I started paying more attention to my finances which was the scariest part to decipher. I beefed up my investments and started becoming more financially wise and astute. There are all kinds of financial programs, calculators, books, websites and a host of other vehicles and advice for how to determine your financial stability during your retirement years. It can be scary and quite complicated. If you follow all the advice out there, it can be overwhelming, confusing and you will never feel secure enough to retire. You will keep right on working until you fall dead on the job – quite literally. This actually happened at my work site. One of the nicest guys on the job began to have heart problems and started going in and out of the hospital. After such health episodes he would return to work not looking too well. Since he had thirty plus years on the job, I asked him why he didn't just go ahead and retire. He told me that he had just two more years on the job before he could get his full retirement pension. Just two more years he said. He didn't make it. He fell dead on the job at his desk. That unfortunate situation harnessed my resolve and I became even more determined not to wait any longer to start this next chapter in my life.

Financial comfort is a big part of my retirement scenario. I have seen too many of my friends retire only to get back into the work world, not because they were bored or needed something to do, but because they needed the money. Statistics show that only 38% of Americans nearing retirement age are actually ready for retirement. That's almost six out of every ten people who are not financial ready to cut the umbilical cord of traditional work.

When I retired I wanted my retirement income to be enough for me to only return to work because I wanted to. So, the scariest part of retirement for me was the money, the financials. I had a certain lifestyle that I wanted to maintain. I'm not rich, not poor but comfortable. I wanted to be able to travel when I so desired and ~~to~~ occasionally be able to buy things that I did not need. I wanted to be able to still contribute to causes and charities that I respected without going broke or negatively impact my financial stability. Also, maintaining my financial independence was a top priority for me in during my retirement years. All of the financial advice was overwhelming and I did not know where to start. I continued to read that you needed to have a certain percentage of your current income in order to retire comfortably. The most common figure is between 60% and 85%, taking into consideration inflation and the increased cost of living. As I mentioned earlier, there is an abundance of information on the financial aspects of retirement. One of my favorite television commercials is the one where the man comes on and asks, "What do you see yourself doing after you retire, 3 months, one year or five years from now?" The commercial then goes on to advertise that they can help you organize your life financially for a secure retirement. Financial management in retirement is not something to be taken lightly. My background and environment did not teach me about planning for retirement so retirement planning was never on my radar screen. Day-to-day living, paycheck to paycheck survival and trying to keep a job while also trying to get a promotion only allowed for perhaps a little bit of savings in a rainy day fund. Putting away money for college was unheard of, let alone planning and savings for retirement. Good jobs were those with a pension based on longevity. Your retirement savings plan was social security and we all know what that means.

Fortunately for me, as a knowledge based seeker who has always been interested in financial security, I became a saver, not a retirement saver, just a saver. Savings for a down payment on a house and for college educations for my sons became the major reasons for savings besides an emergency fund for unexpected expenses. I learned later that it is best to start savings for retirement before your kids' college if you cannot do both simultaneously. The rationale is that your children can always get financial aid assistance in grants, scholarships and educational loans; however, no one is going to give you a loan, grant or scholarship to retire. Nevertheless, I started paying more attention to my finances so I put in place mechanisms to catch up as much as possible in order to comfortably retire. However, the best advice that I received was from a lady that I met at a conference. She told me to calculate how much income I would have once I retired and to begin to manage my expenses to live off whatever that income would be. I did that. I cut back. I downsized. I started buying less and purchasing differently. I got rid of unnecessary superfluous expenses and lived off my "retirement income" for a year. And voila, it worked.

I do believe we should save and invest as much as we can as soon as we can in preparation for retirement but I do not believe that we should be so financially afraid that we continue to literally work ourselves to death. You know, when the policy makers created social security in the 1930's after the great depression, they simply did not expect us to live long enough to collect the benefits. Well, all of that has changed. People are living longer and are in better health. In order to fully enjoy a certain standard of living and quality of life you must be financially solvent. What fun is it if you cannot afford the amenities and luxury that comes with reinventing yourself? Our financial house must be in order to fully enjoy ourselves during our best years.

Lifestyle

Now that we have our health and finances in order the fun part can begin. We get a chance to create and design how we want live the second half of our wondrous years. It's strictly our choice. For many people, retirement is scary. It's the end of the road for them. They succumb to the rocking chair with the remote in hand to do nothing mentally or physically that gives them the joy and happiness to wake up every day with new found vigor and enthusiasm. Others of us will pack up and relocate to the nearest golf course with our beloved spouse. For others, retirement is so unwanted and feared that they continue to work in a traditional environment even when they no longer have to or want to because they have not made plans for life after work, among other reasons.

Retirement, for me, is a new beginning. It is a great new adventure, a promising journey of higher altitudes and a refreshing perspective for a more joyful, burden-free lifestyle. I am not saying that retirement is the road to a perfect life or a utopia of fun and leisure. As human beings we will experience ups and downs, joy and pain and trials and tribulations as a part of our everyday existence. However, retirement provides us with an opportunity to reinvent ourselves and our lives. One of the greatest things about retirement is the freedom of choice that it brings. For me, my retirement meant a new kind of freedom. It meant that I no longer had a boss, there was no one that I had to answer to, no one controlled my time and no one told me where I had to be, when I had to be there or how long I had to stay. Yes, to me retirement was the ultimate freedom to make my own choices as to how I wanted to live this new life.

There are a million-and-one things that I have always wanted to do. One of those things of course, was traveling, as it is for most retirees, but I did not wait until retirement to start doing it. I've already been to 45 states in the US, including Hawaii. I've also visited China, South Africa, Hong Kong, Paris, Canada, South America and many others. I always said that I wanted to travel while I had the energy and stamina to do so. So at this point, I will expand my travels because those who travel know that traveling is one of the best educational experiences that one can experience. However, travel is only one of the myriad of things that I really want to do. I am so excited about the possibilities. Let me repeat. It's now time to create, design and envision this transitional moment of freedom named "retirement".

The question that most people ask is, "what's next?" The other side of that same coin is "what's not next?" The sky truly is the limit and though you may not be able to do everything, you certainly can do what your heart truly desires. I plan to learn a second language, get a paralegal degree to start a new business and become a motivational speaker. There are numerous educational opportunities for baby boomers and seniors to return to school. The Road Scholar (also known as Elderhostel) offers opportunities to learn and travel. There are numerous volunteer opportunities to give back to the community. The internet provides a wealth of resources if you wish to experience a traditional volunteer experience here at home or even in another country. I have always volunteered in the community, even as a young girl. I've freely given time, money and knowledge to a number of causes and charities whose work I've admired. I will continue to do so in my retirement . However, for now, because I love my very flexible schedule and sometimes like getting up in the morning with absolutely nothing on my agenda, I am not inclined to have a strict schedule where I again have to be somewhere at a certain time. That is not for me. However, there are still opportunities that fit my current lifestyle.

Where you decide to live greatly impacts your new retirement lifestyle as well. Are you tired of shoveling snow and wish to relocate to a warmer community? Are you inclined to move closer to a cultural haven, into a city, the country or to another country? There are-plenty of resources to assist in this endeavor. There are annual "best places to retire" publications and even psychological tests to help you make the best decision about where you want to live. I have decided to have dual residency between the east and west coasts because both offer amenities that I enjoy and I intend to take full advantage. Whatever lifestyle you choose, it should be as varied as the Rio's Carnival buffet in Las Vegas which covers a football field. Do something different and try something new. Create and live the lifestyle that you have always wanted. It's really easier than you think. The most difficult part is deciding to take the risk. It's better to weigh the risk with some logic but you won't always want to wonder what could have been. If you have a dream or goal that you want to pursue, by all means, do so. As the saying goes, "You do not want to die with the music still inside of you." Go for it and do it now!

Relationships

Another important ingredient of a successful retirement is your relationships with family, distant relatives, friends and acquaintances. If you are married you have to take into consideration the needs and concerns of your spouse, especially if they are still in the workforce but even more so if you are retiring together. As Robert Browning's poem says, "grow old with me, the best is yet to be". This can be an exciting time for both of you if it is planned right. Many women have been in failing or disappointing marriages for far too long and statistics show that many choose to dissolve their marriages during their retirement. They really do want to start anew. Other women upon, entering retirement, look forward to becoming grandmothers and /or spending more time with their grandchildren. One of my friend's grown children were quite disappointed when she retired because her children expected her to be available more often to babysit. Instead, she expanded her travels and was not as available as they expected. Compromises had to be made to keep the peace. Some friends who are still working may want you to become their "errand runner" since they think you are available or have the time. Relatives who you do not particularly care for may think that you are now available to visit more often. These kinds of sticky situations can be sensitive and will need to be worked out. Your time and certainly who you spend your time with will have to be considered. You do want to spend time with those you love but this is your time and it will call for some new negotiations. The quality of your relationships during retirement can certainly enhance or detract from your peace of mind. You will find that some of your relationships with former work colleagues will change. Make some new friends and renew old friendships. Develop some new acquaintances. I intend to spend more time in a mentoring and coaching role with a group of young woman. A few of these young women have lost their mothers and are seeking guidance and advice as they maneuver their life's journey. I've been through what many of these young women are now going through and we can serve a purpose in each other's lives. Decide the kind of relationship you want with the special people in your life and enjoy these to the utmost.

Legacy

One of the things that we consider as we enter into or while we currently enjoy this retirement phase is the kind of legacy that we want to leave. I believe in the adage that, "Service is the rent we pay for our time here on Earth." We have to ask ourselves what impact we want to leave on the world. Will we leave the world a better place because we were here? I'm sure that you have all heard of the exercise where you pretend that you are at your own funeral or memorial service and then you write what it is that you would like for people to say about you upon your exit from this world. I never liked this idea because I don't have any desire to write my own obituary. However, there are other ideas on how to approach the subject of how you want your life to be and then determining what you would like to have said about you. This method uses the alternative framework of writing the next chapter of your life. You are the main character. You write the script, you set the stage, the scene, the acts, your co-stars, stage hands and production equipment that you may need in the movie called life. I like this idea because it's based on positive creativity and desire rather than doom and gloom. So what do you want this scenario to be like? What do you want this story to say about you? What outcome do you want to produce in this final chapter of life? One of my passions is empowering other women to be successful. I take great joy in seeing other women succeed. My mother was my inspiration because she was the neighborhood go-to Mom for other women who were struggling and trying to raise families. My mother was the perfect example of how to improve your life. She went back to school to further her education, owned three homes during her lifetime and retired early. She provided the very best for her family. In her honor, we have established the Anise Newton Institute for Self-Empowerment, (ANISE,Inc.) a non-profit organization that seeks to empower women during life's trials and tribulations. We have also endowed a scholarship in her name to help provide financial assistance to women pursuing a degree in the field of nursing. Our ultimate goal is to establish a retreat center for women in the sand hills of North Carolina. This is the legacy that we want to live and leave.

In conclusion, I would be remiss if I did not state that in order to live our best life to our highest potential, we must have a spiritual foundation that is all encompassing. Giving thanks, glory and gratitude to the Creator of the Universe, the Almighty God, for blessing us with all that we need to be the best that we can be adds to the joy of creating these most glorious and wonderful years of life. There are numerous resources, guidance and advice to assist you with the power to reinvent yourself and be the best that you can be. The second half is all about your choices, your freedom to decide how you want to be and who you want to be. This is your moment. This is your time. More power to you. Happy Reinvention! Happy Retirement!

Anise Key Brown

Recommended Reading

How to Love Your Retirement-Your Guide to the Best of Your Life; edited by Barbara Waxman

The Joy of Retirement- Finding Happiness, Freedom and the Life You Have Always Wanted by David C. Borchard with Patricia A. Donohoe

The New Retirement-The Ultimate Guide to the Rest of Your Life by Jan Cullinane and Cathy Fitzgerald

I'm Retiring, Now What?! by Hope Egan and Barbara Wagne

Notes:

ABOUT THE AUTHOR

Ms. Carolyn Y. Johnson

Carolyn Johnson co-owns 'Swagg'n2000 LPC, (Doing Something I Believe I Can!). She and her partner conduct workshops throughout the state of New Jersey reaching out toward the Youth. The most rewarding topic being taught to the Youth is Self-Esteem. Ms. Johnson has been certified by The Professional Woman Network, as a Professional Youth Coach.

Ms. Johnson's knowledge of business and professionalism is supported by working with non-profit and charity base organizations. She has over fifteen years of experience working in the Public and Private Sector, as well as three years with Juveniles in a Juvenile Detention Facility.

Among her many accomplishment Ms. Johnson has co-authored "The Power of Change." (Reinventing Yourself At Any Age). She hold a Bachelor of Science Degree (2012), in Information Systems, from Rutgers University, State of New Jersey in addition to Certificates in Gang Recognition in United States.

Book

The Power of Change. Reinventing Yourself At Any Age

Certifications

Certified Professional Youth Coach
State of NJ Commission Juveniles Justice
State of NJ Criminal Justice Police Commission

Professional Organizations

The Professional Woman Network
NJDA JJC
IEEE

Contact:
306 Stockton Avenue
Roselle, New Jersey 07203
Email: Swagg'n2000@aol.com

NINE

A Second Chance: Starting Over After Failure

By Carolyn Johnson

A Second Chance

Have you ever been in a bad situation and you wished it never happened? While you were in that situation did you say, "Why me?" and wonder why this occurred when everything else in your life was going well? Suddenly you wish you had never been born. Yet deep down you may be thinking, "I wish I had a second chance." Well you do! It has been said, "The most important thing you can give anyone in life is a chance."

People of all ages find themselves in bad situations time after time. Failure is not discriminatory! I want you to know you are not alone and that as long as you live you will always have an opportunity for a second chance. At times you may be limited, but the opportunity is still a given.

First, you need to know there are some situations in life you can control and some you can't control *just yet*. As you go though life you have to be positive in your thinking and be very positive with your actions.

So you think, "Why did I do that?" You may have made a poor decision because of selfish reasons such as trying to gain more money, fit in with your peers or wanting status symbols (i.e. a larger home, fancier car, designer clothing, expensive shoes you could not afford) to lift your self-esteem and provide 'bragging rights'. So, you were willing to make wrong decisions just to keep up with your image. And now, you feel all hope is lost because you are near bankruptcy, overdrawn in your bank account and falling behind on home and car payments. You find yourself at the bottom and wishing for a second chance, but wondering if it is possible. Being at the bottom isn't always a bad place to be. Let's just say you are in the right place for now because you can learn something powerful about yourself and you need to reflect upon how you can regain your self-esteem, stop over-spending and rebuild your credit.

At times it can be hard for you to accept the situation you are in because you don't quite understand the choice you made that put you in that predicament anyway. Well, guess what? It is time to forgive yourself and create a new plan of action to stop the negative self-sabotaging behavior and realize that 'things' aren't really giving you status in the world. These 'things' have taken you to the bottom of the well. You have a second chance to change your life!

You may have known or even heard about someone who has been through really rough times in life but somehow that person picked themselves up and started over in life. If failure had never existed, life would've been great for them, right? I'm not so sure! Sometimes we must all be challenged in life, and it is what we have learned from these experiences that really matter. Each of us has the opportunity to begin again! But you need to believe you CAN do this and be willing to work at it.

So you are thinking, "I need that same help!" But there's no one who will listen to you because of your situation. Well, just listen to this—being a failure isn't good for anyone! And it's easy to buy into the "I Can't Do It Syndrome"! Okay. Now it's time to turn your life around and focus on your dreams that are attainable without either overspending, lying, staying in a toxic relationship or setting yourself up for another failing relationship! Oh! Did I hear you say that you don't have any dreams, or you don't believe you can be successful? Well maybe you need to be re-introduced to yourself and follow these two steps which will begin to reveal what you REALLY want in life. Are you prepared to live for success? Okay. You will need two sheets of paper and a pencil or pen to write with. Let begin!

Step #1

Complete your name below:

____

When you think about yourself, what is the first word that comes to mind?

____

Close your eyes and envision yourself as you are now. Embrace your inner self and take pride in the person you are. Yes, you have had failures but you are ready to achieve SO much! Realize how very important you are to yourself, others whose lives you've touched, and know that there's only ONE of you in the world. You are important! Write down all the strengths, gifts and talents you possess.

My gifts, talents and strengths:

1. ______________________________

2. ______________________________

3. ______________________________

4. ______________________________

5. ______________________________

Step #2

Write down the different situations you have found yourself in that have been challenging and in many cases, you have failed (or are failing):

Situation	How Do You Feel About It?

Reflect upon what decisions and choices you have made that led to these failures or challenging situations. What can you do to turn your life around and provide a second chance to yourself?

(i.e. counseling for a failing marriage, job change because of abusive boss, etc.) It is up to YOU to turn your life around. If you wait for others to make decisions for you, their choices are not YOUR choices. Think deeply about what matters to you, chart a new course, then learn to forgive yourself (and others) for your failures. Time to move on to a new beginning.

To begin again, you must be filled with optimism and a positive attitude. You CAN change your life! Here's a list of encouraging thoughts you should try to remember daily from Buzzle.com:

- "*You can do anything you wish to do, have anything you wish to have, be anything you wish to be.*"—Robert Collier
- "*If you think you can, you can. And if you think you can't, you're right.*"—Henry Ford
- "*Success is a state of mind. If you want success, start thinking of yourself as a success.*"—Dr. Joyce Brothers
- "*Age is no barrier. It's a limitation you put on your mind.*"—Jackie Joyner-Kersee
- "*Do what you can, where you are, with what you have.*"—Theodore Roosevelt
- *"Whatever the mind of man can conceive and believe, it can achieve."—Napolean Hill*
- *"Instead of giving myself reasons why I can't, I give myself reasons why I can."* - Author Unknown

- *"When the world says, 'Give up,' Hope whispers, 'Try it one more time.'"*—Author Unknown
- *"People may doubt what you say, but they will believe what you do."* —Lewis Cass
- *"For true success ask yourself these four questions: Why? Why not? Why not me? Why not now?"*—James Allen
- *"Success is simple. Do what's right, the right way, at the right time."* —Arnold H. Glasgow
- *"Success means having the courage, the determination, and the will to become the person you believe you were meant to be."* —George Sheehan

Hopefully you believe you can have a second chance. That you know the opportunity does exist and it's time for you to accept the word "Change" which simply means to become different, or make something or somebody different. After you are willing to accept change into your life, your situations or circumstances will become better as you consistently work on creating a new life. The dreams and goals you once had will become active in your life again once you have let your past failures become history. We ALL have failed at something! Dust yourself off, learn your lessons, and learn to dream again!

Dreams

Did you ever said to yourself as a child "When I grow up I want to be a teacher, fireman, doctor, lawyer, dancer or I want to work for a Fortune 500 company, or the government?" You had a dream didn't you? Well, it's time to rekindle your dreams. If you haven't reach your goals and lifetime dreams, it is time to make a change!

For now, make a commitment to put yourself first! Make yourself a priority as you chart your course to achieve your dreams. Learn to surround yourself with people who believe in you! They are probably aware of your failures but will be overjoyed when they watch you turn your life around and dream of the future again! Become friends with others who have learned to dream again. Be filled with the belief that you CAN turn your life around again and achieve success! Believe in yourself and your abilities.

As you move in the right direction toward your goal, remember this quote by Carol S. Batey. "*We have to forgive ourselves and not hold onto the failure.*" Just remember your three D's: **Desire, Determination, Destiny.**

Each day you will need to take another step toward your goal, even if they are baby steps! Think of yourself running in a marathon and you need to get to the finish line. You will, but you cannot give up in spite of what comes your way. You know you have to finish the race and keep moving until you are living your dream. (Yes, there will be hurdles and obstacles to overcome, but stay focused and believe you CAN reach the finish line!)

You will have to encourage yourself a lot. When finally you let go of your failure, some negative individuals just may wish to remind you of your failings. Remember, don't buy into the 'naysayers' of life. Each human has failed before at something! You do NOT need to be reminded of your past. Leave your ball and chain behind! But do always remember the lessons learned by whatever caused you to fail, whether it was your marriage, bankruptcy, foreclosure, or losing your job!

List what you have learned from your personal or professional failure:

1. ______________________________

2. ______________________________

3. ______________________________

As you begin the steps to achieve your dreams and prepare to cross the 'finish line,' you need to applaud yourself for recognizing the changes you are making in your life. Go on! Celebrate every step of the way. You need to become your own cheerleader! Learn different ways to reward yourself when you stay on track. Remember, this is your second chance! Continue to believe in yourself on a daily basis.

You, the Role Model

When you achieve your dream, goal or success in life, remember the importance of reaching out to others. You were given another chance after falling, and always remember that there are others who really need your help in picking themselves back up. Judge not, of course. Whatever has taken them down, be thoughtful and caring just as you would have hoped someone would have supported you in your darkest hours. Reaching out to others and reminding them of their second chance is an important gift to give someone else. Remind them of your own personal journey and your past fears. Let them know that you conquered these fears by learning to believe in yourself and learning self-forgiveness. You be the role model for others.

No matter what life brings you in the future, to take risks does involve the potential for failing. But without risks, there cannot be big successes. Reflect upon your decisions every step of the way in the future, lead with your heart and mind, and always know that no matter what happens, you will always have another chance! May you enjoy your new life.

ABOUT THE AUTHOR

Andrea Williams

Andrea Williams has been an advocate for women and children for twenty+ years, working with organizations that promote the wellbeing of children and their families who may be at risk. Ms. Williams is currently a Health Services Administrator with the Maryland Prison Systems. Ms. Williams is currently volunteering with the internationally recognized "Girls on the run", a twelve week after school program that is a non profit prevention program that is a life changing character development program for girls 8-12 through a combination of running, lessons and community service. The completion of this program involves the girls running a 5k race.

Ms. Williams in the process of launching a full service consulting practice, which will specialize in workshops, seminars, coaching and programming for teenagers and young adult women to assist them with finding their purpose and passion. As an active member of the professional Women's Network (PWN), Ms. Williams specializes in Women's Issues, Entrepreneurship and leadership training.

Ms. Williams is available for workshops, seminars, keynote addresses, speaking engagements and organizational coaching within the United States and abroad for corporations, organizations, schools, churches and small businesses.

Contact:
Andrea J. Williams, M.B.A, M.S
P.O. Box 4354
Upper Marlboro, MD 20775
888.301.8780

TEN

Fabulous Forties

By Andrea Williams

There was a time when I thought that being forty was a "fate worse than death." I used to think that anyone over nineteen was ancient. Then the years continued to creep up on me and life continued to get better and better, thus the realization that my forties have been the best years of my life. My twenties were my years of getting my feet wet and trying to figure it out. My thirties were the "OK, I have it figured out, but what am I supposed to do" years. And then the forties came and I had an epiphany... This is my life and I am going to take it by the "horns" and begin to live it to the fullest.

Finding Myself

I had always been in a state of flux. I was living, but I wasn't alive. Most of the time, I wasn't sure if I was coming or going. I was angry most of my life. Angry because I was short, my name began with an "A", and angry because I didn't get "this or that." Just angry L. Looking back now, it was a lot of wasted time and energy. It took a lot of soul-searching to rise above and be the "whole" person that I needed to be. I eventually had to be true to myself and understand that I could not be everything to everybody. The word "no" became a new word in my vocabulary. Not to be selfish, but to pamper and take care of me was what was needed to be able to look in the mirror and like who I saw. Finding myself involved, taking a "no holds barred" approach and realizing that I am far from perfect, but who I am is who God intended me to be and at the end of the day… everything is alright.

Opening Up

I didn't know that my forties would be the time of my life when I would be happiest, have more clarity and realize that this is a new beginning, but when I began to come into the moment of realizing this amazing fact, life became a calmer, enjoyable venture. I was always the 'quiet one,' so talking to others about myself was not a common occurrence. I was very private and didn't disclose too much information to many people. I am not sure if it was because I am an only child and I never had to share my thoughts or feelings. But, as I became older, it became clear that opening up and letting people in was a healthy, constructive thing to do. It allowed people not to assume who I am, but see the real me.

Reinventing Myself

During this wonderful time of my life, I have had the opportunity to become a bigger, better me. I have taken on tasks that I would have never done 10 to 15 years ago. Reinventing yourself is different than finding you. If you don't know who you are, how can you take the steps to be a "better you." I would have never gone to dinner and a movie by myself. I have opened up and taken the leap to meet new and exciting people. I joined a cause to end Leukemia and Lymphoma and was involved in a fund raiser that involved running a half marathon. I have never pushed myself that hard to complete anything out of my element like that, but when I was done, I took the bumps and bruises and shined with having completed such a major accomplishment. I completed a second Master's degree to explore another avenue of interest. This time the pressure was off, because it was not a necessity, but a personal development type of goal for me and it helped to solidify my interests.

What new tasks or challenges have you taken on in the last five years?

1. ______________________________

2. ______________________________

3. ______________________________

4. ______________________________

5. ______________________________

Time Out

Really taking the opportunity to savor my forties has been a journey. Realizing that we are only here once and this is no dress rehearsal has given me the energy to really look at taking time out of myself and understanding that "ME" time is also part of the plan. Sometimes taking time out may be taking a "mental health" day off from work. It could be getting a pedicure after work. It could be taking a long walk and really enjoying the view. Whatever it is that allows you to rejuvenate. I did not realize this simple ritual in my twenties and thirties because my priorities were different. During that time period, everything was about everyone else; not about taking care of me. I call this decade the "microwave society." Everything needs to be done quickly and if you always function in that mode, you become stressed and everything is a stressor. Sometimes looking at ways to decrease the stress and create a stress plan will help you conquer some of the added burdens. I am a visual person so seeing information in black and white helps me to really dissect what is going on.

Developing a stress plan, helps you to see what the stressors are (the triggers) and put in a plan to de-stress. Get your journal out and make a commitment to identify the solutions to the following questions:

- Reducing stress is important to me because

____

- My stress is caused by

____

- Some things I can do that would help me feel better are

____

- Some ways I could take care of myself are

____

- A major source of my stress in my life is

____

- I will ask ________________________ to help me stay on track.

Youthful Presence

Not taking life so seriously has been a life-saver for me. Staying young and vibrant is vital not only in my mind and body, but also my spirit. Finding the peace and taking the journey to be happy can happen at any age, but "coming of age" in my forties has been the beginning of making my happiness a priority. Planning and implementing new and creative ideas has been amazing. My adventures have slowly, but surely presented me with the joy that had been missing from my life for so long. My life during my twenties and thirties had been career driven, not life driven. After so long working in such a state, you have no choice but to eventually deflate.

What is it that keeps you young?

____

____

What is it that steals your joy?

____

____

Live Your Joy

I knew that something was missing and it was my spiritual life. I had dabbled in religion, but never really took the plunge to do what I needed to do fully. I would go to church every couple of months, but be sad when things didn't go well. It was because I did not have an understanding of my faith. I began to go to church more, connected with like-minded people and felt a spiritual exploration like no other time in my life. I felt like I could finally exhale and it has been great getting to know God, my creator. None of this could or would be possible without Him.

Finding my joy also entailed creating my prosperity list. Initially, I wasn't sure of how I wanted to tackle all of the things that would make me happy or enjoy doing. I came up with creating the "alphabet game." I took my journal and wrote out the alphabet. Next to each letter I put something that I wanted to do before it's too late. For example, for "M", I put marathon and funny enough, I took the plunge and completed a ½ marathon in 2009. For the letter "W", I decided to connect with like minded professional women and wrote a chapter in two separate books. Never in my life did I think that I would be a published author. I am more of a listener, so writing was "right up my alley." Putting my thoughts and ideas on paper and liking the outcome was powerful for me.

I have discovered a great way to pamper myself and bring myself joy. My birthday is April 18th, so each month on the 18th I plan something special for myself, be it a pedicure, manicure, dinner out or anything that makes me feel special. This is my gratitude to myself and to celebrate. It gives me a boost and helps me celebrate the wonderful life that I have.

List things for which you are grateful.

1. ______________________________

2. ______________________________

3. ______________________________

4. ______________________________

List the things in life that give you joy.

1. ______________________________

2. ______________________________

3. ______________________________

4. ______________________________

Find Your Purpose and Passion

For some reason, fear immobilized me to take the plunge and things that I wanted to do became impossible. I always wanted to open a business and create a program for transitional-aged youth who are at risk. I finally got the guts to make it happen. I finally gained the confidence to show the world what I have to offer. I have found not only my purpose, but my passion.

What is your purpose? What have you been put on this earth to accomplish?

____

____

____

What is your passion? What are the things that drive you?

____

____

____

Turning forty was like a "rite of passage" for me. It was the beginning stages of shedding the old and coming forth as a new person, ready to take on the world. Five years have passed since that new chapter began. I wouldn't change this period of my life for anything in the world. The key to making it a successful process is to release and enjoy the process. I have friends who turned thirty and for months "life was over." Surprisingly, I am the envy of my younger friends who still can't figure it out. Now I can say "forty-something" with pride and feel excited about each new day. If it is this good now, people better watch out when my fifties hit. F-O-R-T-Y is the new twenty and every day is to be enjoyed. Yes, there will be some "valley experiences" but if you push through, your forties, fifties and the rest of your days can be an awesome experience. Life is what you make it, so why not make it FABULOUS?

Complete the box below with goals and dreams you wish to accomplish in your forties (or that you accomplished when you were in your forties)!

FORTIES ARE FABULOUS

ABOUT THE AUTHOR

Toni Kemp

Toni Kemp is employed by The Africa Program, a program whose mission is to promote business, educational, and technological relations between Africa and the State of Texas. She is also a seasoned blogger and has her own website, "Dear World, Love Toni."

She has always had a skill for writing. She started writing short stories at the young age of 8 and attended Rosa Parks High School of The Performing Arts, where her major of focus was creative writing. After graduating from the University of Texas at Arlington with a Bachelor of Arts in English, she decided to begin her blogging career.

As a divorced single mother of one, Toni Kemp is always ready to share her story and experiences to others searching for advice on life in general, from motherhood to life after divorce. She currently resides in Arlington, TX.

Contact:
Toni Kemp
dearworldlovetoni@gmail.com
www.dearworldlovetoni.com
817-235-7254

ELEVEN

Until Death Do Us Part! Recovering After Divorce

By Toni Kemp

As common with young girls, I had a dream about what my wedding one day would be like. On occasion, I thought about the marriage itself. But in my mind, I believed that that was going to be the easy part. The hard part? Choosing the dress. Deciding who I wanted to stand up with me. Picking the ever important wedding colors. Making a guest list of friends and family who were chosen carefully, as to not offend anyone.

And then the time finally came in my life when I was engaged. I was engaged after dating for six months. The wedding was another year out. During that time I took control of the wedding plans like a captain to his ship. I made a list of "To Dos", with timelines from twelve months out to the day of the wedding. I worked to keep my small budget even smaller, but making sure the wedding looked like a priceless masterpiece. I joined TONS and TONS of wedding sites, watched every wedding show I could, and filled up my wedding binder with items, vendors and wedding contracts.

But it wasn't all about just the ceremony and reception. My fiancé and I went to premarital counseling with my pastor. During our dating period we talked about an endless list of topics, from favorite movies, to childhood stories, to plans for the future. Even my pastor commented on how diverse our conversations must have been, to be able to answer all of his questions with the words, "We've actually talked about this before."

Then the big day arrived. All the months of planning, endless hours of assembling wedding favors, all the ideas that I had in my head had finally been created into this special day. And it was almost everything I wanted it to be. Of course, as with most wedding days, there were things that went wrong or that were unexpected but I was surrounded by friends and family and was happy. Once we left the wedding reception that night, I was confident that we tackled one of the hardest days in our life together with ease. Everything else should be pretty much a piece of cake, right?

Wrong. Over time, it seemed that all those things we talked about before the wedding really weren't enough. Things that we could look at objectively before being married and solve with talking and perspective changes became strains in our marriage with the words, "You never listen to me!" peppered throughout. And before you know it, the life that we thought we had planned out with ease fell from our grasp.

Before getting married, tons of advice gets thrown your way. Sometimes wanted, other times forced upon you. Lots of people will have words of advice and tidbits to help you through what they already know you will go through. But what happens when the marriage is over? No one really gives advice for that part. And if you are in this new world called "divorced," I don't even have advice to offer. What I DO have are stories of my experience and lessons I've learned along the way. As with most things, I won't say that I'm an expert in this. I'm just one woman, who hopes to share my stories with you, and believes you can take away something from this. At the very least, read this and know right now that you are NOT alone in this. You have at least one person who can truly say they understand and know what's going on in your mind right now. So let my life lessons be your guide to get through this new time in your life.

The Guilt

Probably the hardest lesson that I've learned is that you will feel guilt. And even now, three years from the separation, two years from the divorce, it's still there. At times you don't expect you will ask yourself, did I really try hard enough? Perhaps I really was the problem; is there any way to fix me? If I meet someone else, am I going to fall into the same traps and end up here again? And the biggest guilt-loaded question that ran through my head most often? Is God angry at me? Has He shunned me?

Guilt settled in heaviest immediately after the separation. It was common practice for me to put my daughter down for the night, climb into my bed and cry myself to sleep. I did well to appear happy and put together in front of family and friends. I even had people come to me and tell me that they admired the way I was handling everything. My closest friends admired my strength during this time; I was even called a "shero" by a dear friend. But they didn't know of the pain and burden I felt every night when I laid down in silence. In the dead of night, alone in the darkness, the loudest voice in my head would clearly yell out, "Why didn't you try harder? You were supposed to be different, not a statistic."

The truth in this lesson is that you will continue to feel guilt. But you don't need to be burdened with that all of your life. People are human. We aren't perfect. We expect perfection from imperfect beings and always end up getting hurt. Know that there is a reason for everything in this world. If not for my marriage, I wouldn't have the world's most beautiful and amazing four year old as a daughter. I wouldn't trade anything for her. If not for my marriage, I wouldn't have become this incredibly strong woman who learned how to tackle bills and parenting with one hand tied behind my back. And if not for my marriage, I would not have learned how much I am loved by God. It's true that God hates divorce. But He does not hate divorcees. He continues to bless me day after day. He lets me know that it's okay that I fell short of what He wanted, but that He will not leave me and has big things in store for me. And if He is ok with me and doesn't hold the failed marriage over my head, why should I continue to punish myself?

The Burden

Another lesson that I've learned is there will always be people who think the problem was that you didn't try hard enough. Some may even tell you face to face that you simply were being lazy and not investing the true time it takes to make a marriage work. Family and friends both will ask if you'd tried counseling. If you really REALLY tried it and not just went through the motions. They'll ask if you talked to your pastor or spiritual counselor. They'll ask if you really talked and listened to each other and tried everything. They will give you the name and number of a counselor that they know and will insist that you call them. You'll get emails from friends and article after article about reconnecting and counseling. You'll sometimes get approached by people you don't even know because they've shared your story with others in a desperate act to help you.

I actually did this very same thing to a close friend of mine. At the time, I was unmarried and single. She was in a marriage that seemed to appear less than stellar, to say the least. And in my infinite wisdom I decided that I should go ahead and offer my unsolicited advice because I was a friend that cared and I could look at things objectively and tell her exactly what she needed to do. Therefore, I felt that I knew about how marriage should be. Silly me, right? But I couldn't understand how things could go wrong if you really did put the time and effort into making a change. And I felt, if it didn't work, then you just weren't working hard enough. That of course, if you did work on it honestly, it was going to fix itself.

The truth in this lesson is that you HAVE done everything you could and no one will really understand that. And the only person you can account for during this is yourself. You can't make your spouse do anything. But if you put your all into it, then that's the best you can do. There's no use in getting angry at people for asking this same question over and over. Just smile and let them know that yes, you have but you've come to a mutual agreement about ending the marriage. Or just smile and say thank you. Either way, you can't fault them for caring about you that much. Their intentions are good, even if their delivery is bad. Over time, people will get the message and will leave you alone about it. But just look at it as one of those things that lets you know that your family and friends love you and really want the best for you, in all situations. And isn't it wonderful to know that you and your well being matters so much to so many people?

The Strength

One of the greatest lessons I learned is that I am strong. I thought I knew what strength was before. I had no idea what true strength was like until I found myself as a divorced single parent. All of the trials I experienced in the marriage seemed amplified once I was divorced. The financial difficulties we experienced as a married couple don't compare to the financial difficulties I experience in my divorced state. The tiredness I felt during the marriage from being a homemaker and mother and handling a full time job doesn't compare to the tiredness I feel now with absolutely no one else at the house.

This was something I was familiar with, but as a daughter of a divorced woman. I remember my mother and my sister juggling family time, school time and work time together. But my mother, being the incredible woman she is, never let us feel any of the burdens she felt. She worked hard at keeping a good balance at home and work. But I can now admire and identify how she did it. The weekends we spent visiting Mom's job and helping her get organized at work was another way she worked to stay on top of her game at work. We just saw it as a fun opportunity to see her office and use the photocopier. The evenings we went to the movies were fun times for my sister and me, but my mother spending $3 for us to see movies at the dollar theater was a way to enjoy our time without a heavy financial burden being set down upon us.

The truth in this lesson is you have the power to do absolutely amazing things. It just takes certain situations to bring it out of you. Never in my wildest dreams would I think that I would be able to stay up all night with a sick baby, then turn around and go to work with less than two hours of sleep, just to have to go home and play doctor mommy all over again. Never did I think that I would be able to figure out how to stretch my last few dollars of a paycheck out to make sure my little one and I had a roof over our heads, food in our bellies and gas in the car. I look back over these things and take pride in the things I've been able to do. I don't fear this divorced life as I did when I first started out my journey. I know that I'm going to be able to come through any situation with strength and confidence. And I know that one day my daughter will be able to look back and say those same things about me.

The Future

One lesson that happened to come to me before I was really ready was that once you are divorced, a lot of people will be looking for you to move forward in your love life, even before you send out the signals. Just as you will get advice regarding counseling, you will get questions about when you will start dating again or whether you will ever be married again. People will let you know that they know a nice single man that's available. You'll be invited to speed dating events.

One of the biggest surprises may come from friends who approach you for dates. They may say how they've always taken an interest in you and have been wondering if you would be interested in going out some time. Not only does this make you wonder about whether you are ready to move forward or not, but you also have to think about whether this is will jeopardize your friendship. Some people can successfully navigate the lines of friends versus person of interest.

But even before you get to these deeper questions, the truth you'll find in this is that you will be ready to move forward with your romantic life when YOU are ready. No one can put a time frame on this. The truth is, the ending of a marriage is very much similar to losing a loved one. You need to have a period of time to thoroughly grieve over your loss. You need time to cry about it, to come to terms with it and to let it go without holding onto any grudges or animosity. Only once you've done this can you think about moving forward, in all aspects of life. Especially romantically. Any one that approaches you before you are ready shouldn't be turned away with harsh words or attitude. Just let them know that you are honored and flattered by their interest but that you just aren't ready to move into that phase yet. That's a response that anyone can respect and it very well may help you weed out the interests of people who are true and those who are not. And that's just one less headache to avoid in the long run.

The Ex

If you are divorced with children, you will quickly learn that you will always be connected to your ex for the rest of your life. You won't necessarily have to deal with them on a one-on-one basis daily, but at the very least you will need to maintain constant contact for the good of the children. This also holds true for the extended family of your ex. Having children instantly creates a bond with another person that you will always have, unless there is a reason to cut contact with that person completely.

When I separated from my ex- husband, we worked together to maintain normalcy for our child as much as we could. She was not present the day he actually packed up his things and left. But we worked to establish time for them to spend together every week. She took to the process with ease, always looking forward to those times when she would have "Daddy and Me" time. He would call her in the middle of the week and plan out what kind of activities they would do. She would eagerly give him a list a mile long that ranged from going to the zoo to just reading a book together. I was also grateful to have a chance to have some personal time and get a few things accomplished.

The truth in this lesson is, you must maintain a good relationship with your ex for the sake of your children. No matter how things ended in the marriage, they are first and foremost the father of your child(ren). Of course, if the reason for the marriage ending was something that endangered the life of your child, then you may need to consider how to move forward without them around. Other than that, there's no need to bring up any arguments or hold onto any animosity when dealing with them. After all, if not for them you wouldn't have the amazing child(ren) that you share in the first place. And that alone deserves some amount of gratefulness. Even if what you have to do is only talk to them regarding your child, PERIOD, then do that. Do whatever it takes for you to maintain a happy and healthy relationship with one of the most important people in the life of your child. And believe me, the happiness in your children's eyes when you are sending them to have some one-on-one time with their father is going to be more than enough to convince you that you are indeed headed on the right track.

In the event that you do not have children with your ex, it still behooves you to maintain a positive and healthy relationship with them. Practically, if you have any business or legal responsibilities with them, keeping an open relationship helps to keep the personal side just that and not make it into a public issue. On the personal side, letting go of your anger and showing true forgiveness opens you up to the goodness that life has to offer. You know the saying, "When it rains, it pours." Ever had the feeling that once something goes wrong in your life, that it ALL goes wrong? That's because like forces are drawn to each other. If you're already in a bad mood, you're going to only see bad coming your way. But if you're feeling great, you'll be amazed at all the glorious things life has to offer to you. So let go of the grief, let go of the pain, in order to help you move forward and grow into a brighter future.

These are the things I've learned on my journey thus far. While it seems I've made many accomplishments along the way, I'm still not done. I'm still learning and I'm still moving along. But I'm open to all of the experiences that I've yet to discover. I've let go of the pain and anger. I understand that there isn't anyone to point blame to. I know that for the sake of my life and the sake of my daughter's life, I must keep going forward with a genuine heart and an open mind. I know there is a grand life after divorce and I'm making that life into my very own.

Notes:

ABOUT THE AUTHOR

Elizabeth C. Scott

Elizabeth is employed as a state social worker with The Cabinet for Health and Family Services as an investigator for the Domestic Violence Team. She is also an intern case manager at YMCA Safe Place teen shelter. During her undergraduate studies in social work at the Kent School of Social Work, Elizabeth had the opportunity to study abroad working in Uganda's child welfare system for an entire summer. In May 2010 she earned a Bachelor's degree in Social Work, graduating with Cum Laude Honors. Immediately after graduation she began working towards her master's degree and will obtain a Master's of Science in Social Work (MSSW) in May 2011 as the first person in her family to achieve an advanced degree. She is passionate about social justice and looks forward to fulfilling her role as an advocate.

Outside of work Elizabeth has enjoyed performing with Louisville Entertainment for nearly three years doing stage plays, in addition to appreciating the arts from the audience as one her favorite activities. She has two wonderful children, Nevaeh & Isaiah, who bring her much joy and inspire her daily.

Contact:
Elizabeth C. Scott
(502) 681-6336
Ecscott24@yahoo.com

TWELVE

The Front of the Class: The Power of Education

By Elizabeth C. Scott

"The more you read, the more things you learn, the more places you will go."—Dr. Seuss

Let me begin by stating that my educational journey was not one that was straight and narrow. In fact, I took several detours that included everything from barely graduating from high school, withdrawing during my first year of college, and returning as a single parent of two small children. It has been through my continual pursuit of higher education that I have achieved goals that once seemed impossible. Doors that I never knew existed have opened and I have become the woman I was always meant to be but failed to recognize.

You may be thinking about going back to school, withdrawing from school, or be well on your path to meeting your educational goals. Wherever you are on your journey, this chapter is intended to give you not only a bit of confidence and some tips on how to succeed in the classroom. I also hope to give you some first-hand knowledge and experience to help you make the most out of your time in school.

Finding Your Passion

Many people begin their educational path only to find out that the field of study they have chosen does not suit them. It is fairly common for students to change majors several times. In order to possibly avoid this common pitfall of early education, it is important to take an honest inventory of what you are good at, what you are passionate about, and what career you could envision yourself working in the majority of your life. I suggest avoiding choosing a field of study merely based on financial gain. There are many people who come to work miserable and hate their jobs because they lack a true interest and passion about what they do. Take a moment to think about what you are passionate about and what you are good at. Use the lines below to create a list of things you currently do or have done in the past that you do well and that bring you true happiness. Next, brainstorm possible careers and majors that utilize these interests.

1. ______________________________

2. ______________________________

3. ______________________________

4. ______________________________

5. ______________________________

Regardless of your major there will be general education classes that everyone is required to take. This is a good place to begin because these courses are varied and it is likely that you will prefer one field of study to another. For example, I found that I preferred sociology, history, and psychology over math and science. Through your interactions in the classroom and through your life experiences, your passion will be revealed to you and you will begin to discover your own educational path. If you enjoy what you do, you will do it well! I would also suggest creating a personal mission statement. For more information and instructions on go to: www.franklincovey.com.

Communication

In all facets of life, effective communication is vital. Think about your relationships with other people in your personal life – friends, family, and, significant others – and you can probably recognize those relationships that are problematic by the quality of communication you have with one another. Barriers and road blocks are created by both the lack of and poor quality of communication. The same applies to your professors. If you are not communicating with them, how are they supposed to know how to help you. Or, that you even need help, for that matter. I can almost guarantee that your professors will want you to succeed and do well in their classes. I recommend frequent contact and communication with your professors that includes asking questions during class, dropping by during office hours, sending emails, and making phone contact. (Most professors will usually let you know which of these communication options are available in the first class.) It is essential to start communication early on in the semester. Often, students have disabilities that qualify them for various accommodations that can aid them in their academic success. If this describes you, do not wait. Contact your school's resource center and get the appropriate documentation to your professor so you can get off to a good start. The worst thing a student can do is to wait until he or she is totally confused and off course. Everyone knows that life shows up during the least expected times. Chances are, at some time in your educational career you are going to experience some form of crisis or an unplanned life event. Do not miss class for a valid reason without letting your professor know what is going on in your situation. However, a reason is not the same as an excuse! Sorry, if your dog eats your homework you should be prepared to face the consequence. I am not advising you to divulge all of your personal information to your professor in the event of a crisis, but you should give them a heads up so they will be more willing to work with you. Remember, communication is the key to success in your personal life, in the classroom, and in your career!

Another aspect of communication is advocating for oneself as a student. On many occasions I was able to advocate for myself by communicating my situation in a way that resulted in a higher grade. For example, perhaps you misunderstood an assignment and did not realize it until you got back a less than expected grade. In that situation I would suggest addressing your professor by explaining your misunderstanding and then request an opportunity to make corrections. Your instructor may or may not oblige but at least you have spoken up and made an attempt to improve your grade. Whatever you do, do not approach your professor in a hostile or blaming manner. Humility is vital in this scenario.

Identify Support

Absolutely everything I have accomplished could not have happened without my support network. People need people. The reality is that by simply making the decision and committing to furthering your education, you are taking on a huge challenge. I cannot tell you how many times I relied on my support members to remind me exactly why I was sacrificing my personal time away from my family during the grueling hours I spent doing research and writing papers. Without my support network to remind me that what I was doing served a greater purpose, there were a few times I might not have persevered. It is important to choose the right people to entrust with your educational goals. Unfortunately, we all have people in our lives that would just as soon see us fail than master our goals. Think now of some key people in your life who unconditionally have your back and have the ability to cheer you on during the worst of times. This may include a professor, a counselor, a church member, or whomever you believe has faith in you. Use the spaces below to identify these individuals.

1. ______________________________
2. ______________________________
3. ______________________________
4. ______________________________
5. ______________________________

It is also a good idea to identify those on the other end of the spectrum who I like to refer to as the "Haters." You are making life changes and decisions to better yourself by furthering your education, and it is sad but true that not everyone is going to understand why you are putting so much time, effort, and, money into obtaining a degree. You have to sever ties with these people because they can be toxic dream stealers. There have been relationships that I had to realize I needed to let go of. It is not against them, it is just for *you*. Surround yourself by like-minded people. Seek out those people whose qualities you admire. There is no better way to get to where you want to be than to follow someone who has already paved the path for you. I find it helpful to have a mentor and I suggest that everybody have at least one. You may have already listed this person in your inventory of support members. As you get further along in your journey you will recognize people that you admire and hope to emulate, scholastically and professionally. I have several key people in my life that I look up to and have used for advice and feed back when deciding my next step towards reaching both my academic and career goals.

Time Management

Believe me when I say I understand a busy and chaotic schedule. There have been many occasions when I was overwhelmed and overbooked. The key is to prioritize and strategically plan your schedule. Recognize your strengths and weaknesses when it comes to time management and organization. If you are not a morning person (you know who you are), do not sign up for early morning classes. Do not set yourself up to fail. Keep in mind that afternoon classes fill up first so do not procrastinate when you are registering. Figure out what your ideal schedule is and register for the classes that work best for you. The best advice I can give when it comes to time management is not to spread yourself too thin. The following chart lists four quadrants that will help you prioritize the things you have on your schedule. Your goal is to stay in Quadrants I and II as these consist of IMPORTANT tasks to be completed. Activities represented in Quadrants III and IV are NON-IMPORTANT time robbers that should account for a minimal portion of your time.

The Time Management Matrix – Activities

	Urgent	**Not Urgent**
Important	I • Crises • Pressing problems • Deadline-driven projects	II • Prevention, capability improvement • Relationship building • Recognizing new opportunities • Planning, recreation
Not Important	III • Interruptions, some callers • Some mail, some reports • Some meetings • Proximate, pressing matters • Popular activities	IV • Trivial busy work • Some mail • Some phone calls • Time wasters • Pleasant activities

Based on *7 Habits of Highly Effective People*, Stephen Covey

It is also important to recognize that it is better to be exceptional in a couple areas of interest as compared to being mediocre in several. Put your effort into the areas that you will make the most impact and gain the most knowledge.

Seize The Moment

During your educational career you may run across once in a life time opportunities. Now is the time to take advantage of these experiences. If you have the opportunity to study abroad, as I did, you are in for a life changing event, even if it is just over Spring Break. However, if that is not available, you do not have to travel overseas to learn about other cultures. Remember, you are on a campus with international students. Do not be shy, and introduce yourself. Chances are you could both learn a lot from each other. Make the most of your extracurricular activities, join clubs, participate in sports, or volunteer. Not only does this build leadership and team work, but will also look really nice on your resume and creates exceptional networking opportunities that could be beneficial later on as you enter your chosen field. Oftentimes people overlook school resources. You should go out of your way to access everything available to you as a student. Whether you need tutoring, healthcare, counseling or a multitude of other services, almost everything you need is available on campus. Educate yourself and make use of these free services while you can.

Not So Common Sense

This section is dedicated to the mundane but crucial aspects of succeeding in school. One common temptation is the almighty student loan. Your mind may start racing with thoughts of grandiosity and splendor. You began telling yourself things like, "You should go on a shopping spree with all of that loan money, you know you have needed to redecorate your pad, or, whoo-hoo, Party-time!" I encourage you to quickly pump your brakes and read the fine print! DISCLAMIER: Loans have to be repaid! It is not free money and some student loans even accrue a very high interest rate. My first suggestion is to apply for financial aid. These are government paid funds that are dispensed as grants, which means you are not responsible for repayment. Apply for as many scholarships as you can. Many scholarship opportunities require you to submit an essay with your application and it is a good idea to create a template about yourself, your educational goals, and ambitions. Next, tailor the finer details of your application to fit the specific scholarship you are applying for, building on your basic profile. NOTE: You do not have to accept your entire financial aid award. You have the option to use only what you truly need. If possible, borrow from only subsidized loans – you do not accrue interest on this loan while you are in school. You should also beware of credit cards and spend only what you can afford to pay off at the end of the month. Remember, you are not going to school to get a job so you can spend the rest of your life paying back student loans. In fact, depending on your major, there are scholarship programs that will cover your educational expenses if you agree to be employed by a particular agency after you graduate. It was not until I began my master's program that I ever needed a dime of student loan money because I took advantage of one of these scholarship programs. Another perk to these scholarships is the fact that oftentimes you have a job waiting for you right out of school.

Most importantly, SHOW UP to your classes. You may run across professors who do not have an attendance policy. They are assuming you are responsible enough to make the right decision, plus if you are paying for the course you should at least get your money's worth. Remember, you will only get out of the class what you put into it; this also applies to most areas in life. Be prepared when you show up to class. A minimal requirement of success in school is utilizing your pen and paper. Seriously, you would be surprised of the number of students who actually come to class empty handed. Do not be the classmate who always has to ask, "Can I get a sheet a paper?" Make sure to bring your own supplies. Know the content of the class. It will not only increase your participation, but you might just sound like you know what you are talking about. Completing your reading assignments before class will allow you to make a meaningful contribution to the class and enrich your learning.

Review Your Work

Spell check is the icon at the top of your computer screen, the one with ABC and a blue check mark. This is your friend. I have been guilty of relying on spell check too much and have overlooked words that are grammatically correct but not contextually correct. I suggest printing your paper after spell check to look for the words that may be spelled correctly but are irrelevant or not in the correct place. This is one of the main reasons I requested to submit a "do-over" as a result of the most simple and overlooked errors. Save yourself the embarrassment and get in the habit of reviewing your work in order to submit proficient assignments.

Be Responsible

School is a lot of fun and you are going to meet many new people. However, do not make the mistake of majoring in Partying 101. Yes, this a time in your life that you will learn and try new things – just make responsible decisions.

The facts: Colleges have some of the highest rates of alcohol consumption. Over-drinking can lead a multitude of unintended consequences, not to mention death and potential health problems. Alcohol decreases our inhibitions, decision making abilities, and can be the cause of unintended death and overdose. With alcohol abuse there are the most serious risks of alcohol poisoning and memory loss. However, even moderate alcohol consumption can lead to criminal charges (i.e. driving under the influence, underage consumption, public intoxication, etc.), health problems, lower functioning in all areas, and humiliation. What may have given you the confidence boost you needed at the moment can result in a plethora of unintended consequences you could regret for years.

Do not be fooled by good looks or a hot body. Use protection EVERY time you engage in sexual activity, regardless of who it is with. There are high rates of sexually transmitted diseases and not all can be cured by an injection at the campus health clinic. You cannot judge a book by its cover, just like you cannot look at someone and know if they are infected with HIV or other sexually transmitted diseases. If you are sexually active, know your status and get tested often. You cannot assume you or your partner is disease free. It is not uncommon to present no symptoms of some infections. If you have sex, YOU ARE at risk.

Setting Goals

Have you ever heard that people who write their goals down are more likely to achieve them? The odds of goal completion increase if you read them often and say them out loud or to other people. I believe in the power of speaking things into existence. Mahatma Gandhi said it. *"Your beliefs become your thoughts, your thoughts become your words, your words become your actions, your actions become your habits, your habits become your values, your values become your destiny."* Be specific when writing your goals and create a time line of steps it will take to achieve them. Reward yourself as often as you complete the specific steps to your long-term goal.

Personal Goal Review

Identify what you are currently doing.

____

____

____

What do you want to have accomplished in 1 month?

____

____

____

What do you want to have accomplished in 6 months?

____

____

____

What do you want to have accomplished in 1 year?

____

What do want to have accomplished in 5 years?

What is your long-term goal?

What is your dream goal?

This chapter is dedicated to my children—you are my motivation, to my mother—thank you for your support and encouragement, and to the Family Scholar House for paving the foundation of my educational journey. And to those of you who believed in me and recognized my potential long before I did, you would be proud!

ABOUT THE AUTHOR

LORENE COLLIER PURCY

Lorene Collier Purcy is a Certified Life Coach, International Author & Professional Speaker. She has over 10 years experience as a small business consultant and life coach. Her expertise in these areas, range from business administration to financial management.

Lorene enjoys helping people discover a positive mindset and that they can find balance from their choices integrating personal and business life strategies. She is recognized by colleagues and clients as an accomplished professional with a high degree of personal integrity. Lorene is known for a contagious passion for excellence, a talent for practical business solutions, and has a competence for being a motivational leader.

Raised in Fort Worth, Texas, Lorene lives with her husband, Greg and their three dogs, Rocky, Nhyla, and Kyroz. When she is not working, she loves to read, travel and network.

Contact:
Website: www.nowimliving.com
Email: lorene@nowimliving.com
Facebook: facebook.com/lcpurcy

THIRTEEN

Living the Life You Want NOW!

By Lorene Collier Purcy

I'll bet if I ask you to describe your life right now, you would probably say *busy, stressed*, or *hectic*, meaning that your life lacks balance and is spiraling out of control. Most of us seem to live unbalanced lives while searching for some kind of state of equilibrium. In fact, life balance is one of the most discussed topics in our culture today, and indeed, one of the most elusive. I would like to share with you some ideas about achieving the life you want in spite of living the chaotic life that most of us have come to regard as normal.

The life you want does not start next year, next month or even next week. It starts now. Yes, Today! Today is the only day you have. You may have experienced adversity in your past and have uncertain predictions for your future, but in order for you to live the life you desire you are going to have to get rid of the negative mindset that is holding you back and start enlarging your vision. Once you focus on improving YOU – your attitudes, skills, and philosophies, everything around you will improve (your money, career, relationships, and health). You will begin to see yourself doing more, enjoying more and being more.

In this chapter, I will be revealing to you seven simple principles that you can use to improve your life regardless of where you are today. If you wait, your quality of life and standards will gradually decrease over time until the life you are living does not look anything like the life you want. On the other hand, if you start living the life you want *now*, your quality of life will only improve and get better. So what are you waiting for? It's time to start "Living the Life You Want NOW!"

1 – Give Your Self-Image a Boost.

"People are not disturbed by things but by the view they take of them."
—Epictetus

Self-image is how *you* perceive yourself. Living the life you want now has a lot to do with how you view yourself. Have you ever heard the saying, "Happiness is found within?" Well, as trite as it may sound, it is true. The most important factor to happiness and well-being is your self-esteem or how you perceive yourself.

Take a moment to reflect on the following questions, answering them as truthfully as possible. You will discover a few self-impressions that you may have built up over time. These self-images can be very positive, giving you confidence in your thoughts and actions, or negative, making you doubtful of your capabilities and ideas.

- How do you feel about yourself and what others think of you?
- What do you think and feel about where you are today?
- What limiting beliefs are holding you back from what you want?

Having a positive self-image can be difficult, especially if you are affected by life's hardships, but there are some things that you can do to improve your self-image and self-esteem. These things can, in turn, improve other aspects of your life such as your academic status, financial success, relationships, and even health.

A very important action to changing your self-image is to listen to your internal voice and judgments on how you see yourself. Being aware of self-criticisms can help you determine your current self-image and decide if it needs to be improved. Like improving any skill, improving your self-image takes time, patience and practice.

Developing good self-esteem involves having a positive but realistic attitude toward yourself, the world around you and appreciating your self-worth, while at the same time behaving responsibly towards others. Self-esteem isn't self-absorption, it's self-respect.

There are many ways you can change negative thoughts and self-criticism to more realistic and positive thoughts. Below I have listed just a few positive thought strategies that you can use to remind yourself of these constructive approaches to changing your self-esteem.

- Accept imperfections, flaws and being human.
- Replace criticism with encouragement.

- Don't feel guilty about things beyond your control.
- Focus on what you CAN do, not what you can't.
- Forgive and forget.

By working from the inside out and focusing on changing your own way of thinking before changing the circumstances around you, you can build your self-esteem. The goal of this positive thinking is to give you a more positive self-concept. While accepting yourself and honestly seeing the good in yourself, you will remove the internal barriers that can keep you from living the life you want now!

2 – Determine What Is Important to You.

"It's not what you say or what you intend to do but what you actually do that reveals what is most important to you."—Brian Tracy

Before you can live the life you want, you need to know what the life you want *is.* Determining what is important to you is critical to building life-long success. It is different for everyone. No two people are the same so only you can determine what is important to you.

We fill our lives with so many activities and often place our priorities in things that are not very important to us and will not get us any closer to reaching the goals we set. The challenge is to choose what you do and how you live consciously. The key to living the life you want is to determine what is most important to you in all areas of your life. After answering the following questions, you should be able to establish what you value most and assess those values with how you actually spend your time.

So take a few minutes right now and decide what is most important in your life and your relationships. Make a pact with yourself that when you commit to doing something you will be fully present and fully engaged. Set a family meeting and ask your family members to do the same.

- What is most important to me in my spiritual walk?
- What is most important to me in my relationship with my partner/spouse?
- What is most important to me in my relationship with my kids?
- What is most important to me in my career?

3 – The Power of a Positive Attitude.

"If you don't like something, change it. If you can't change it, change your attitude."—Maya Angelou

A positive attitude is important to your social status, your health, your career, the way you challenge obstacles, and the kind of people you attract. In a world that revolves

around who you know, having a positive attitude will bring more positive opportunities into your life.

A positive attitude can inspire you to get more things accomplished and help you stay on track with your goals. You begin to view what you once thought of as obstacles as learning opportunities. Your energy level expands because negative thoughts don't weigh you down. You live a less stressful life, which can be longer, more enjoyable and filled with satisfaction from your positive outlook.

Wrapping your mind around the positive instead of the negative requires time, commitment and an abundance of patience. You can start by evaluating your thoughts from time to time during the day. If you notice that your thinking is creeping into a negative viewpoint, consider how you might view a particular thought in a more positive way. Remember, the obstacles are no longer obstacles, but become opportunities for you to learn and grow.

4 – Why Set Goals – Do Goals Matter?

"If you want to live a happy life, tie it to a goal, not to people or things."
—Albert Einstein

Have you thought recently about what your goals in life really are? We set them all the time. We set a goal to break a bad habit, a goal to pay off credit card debt, to lose some weight or even a goal to start setting goals. At first you are all excited, you see a little improvement, but over time you get complacent, especially if you do not see instant results.

You might feel as if you are aimlessly wandering in the world. You work very hard, but you do not seem to get anywhere worthwhile. A key reason that you feel this way is that you have not spent enough time thinking about what you want from life, and have not set goals for yourself. After all, would you set out on a major journey with no real idea of your destination? Probably not!

Goal setting is a powerful process for thinking about your ideal future, and for motivating yourself to turn your vision of that future into reality. The process of setting goals helps you choose where you want to go in life. By knowing precisely what you want to achieve, you know where you have to concentrate your efforts. Following are some ideas to get you on your way to setting and accomplishing what you want out of life:

- Create your "big picture" of what you want to do, be and see in your life within the next 20 years, 10 years, in 5 years and even now.
- You will have to realize the importance of why you are setting the goals you want and start working on them daily one step at a time.
- No matter what, stay in the positive. You will experience setbacks, but you must remain focused on your reason for setting the goal in the first place. Decide what you will continue to move forward on, not away from. Focusing on the problem will only hinder your progress, so be aware of the choice of words you use to define your goals and you will start achieving success.

5 – A Model of Success

"A mentor is someone who allows you to see the hope inside yourself."
—Oprah Winfrey

Sometimes you need an expert with specific information, life experience, and advice that will help you move forward. This could be a friend, a family member, a counselor, a mentor, a role model, a coach, or a pin-up picture of someone you admire that you post up on your calendar of success. You need to carefully identify that person who can encourage you, someone who you are close enough to share your goals with and someone who can check your progress and keep you on track.

You will find that some goals you set for yourself are absolutely impossible without the direct help of someone who has been where you are and has experienced what you might be going through. The person you chose to work with is skilled at helping you carefully prepare a plan of action for dealing with obstacles that may come your way.

This person is not only found in face to face situations. You may also find the encouragement you need from reading a book, listening to audio tapes and even from attending a workshop or seminar.

Finding someone to support you may take some time. You should be active in your church and community, building relationships with people who are successfully doing the things you desire to do. The easiest way to be successful in life is to "Model" success. If it's working for them, then it can work for you, too.

6 – What is Your Financial Mindset?

"In all realms of life it takes courage to stretch your limits, express your power, and fulfill your potential… it's no different in the financial realm."—Suze Orman

Most of us have money problems; we learned math, English and history in school, but we didn't learn anything about our personal finances. What we know about personal finance is what we have learned through trial and a lot of error. You should not be ashamed or embarrassed about your money woes. However, you should use that energy to get motivated and make some changes. You, too, can change your financial mindset. Financial freedom is 80% behavior management and 20% math. Your financial mindset requires that you manage yourself, as well as your money. Money does not cure problems; in some cases, it magnifies them. Your quality of life will increase when you make the decision to live within your means and learn how to take control of your financial mindset.

If you want to change where you are *right now*, you have to first change the thoughts you are having about money *right now*. You have to know and trust that things can be different – that you are not locked into your current way of being, your current experience, or your current reality.

We all have the capacity to make a lot of money, even though most of us limit our ability. If you create a strong image of where you are going financially, that vision will give you power. That power will pull you forward into action, which will essentially bring forth the results you initially visualized.

So often you see the results that successful people have, and that is what you focus on. "I want that!" What you miss is that you have to go deeper and look first at the thoughts of that successful person. Learn their language and their actions, because those building blocks are the major factors behind where they are today.

I am certainly not suggesting that you will not experience an occasional period of negativity. But the way you think about your personal finances must be extremely powerful and success oriented for you to be able to take the necessary actions to getting the results you want.

You will need to erase what you have been accustomed to doing, reprogram your mind with the right attitude and start taking control of your money. I know. I had to. It will take time but if you just do a little bit every day you will see amazing results that will get you one step closer to living the life you want now!

7 - Living the Life You Want NOW!

Nelson Mandela said it best: *"There is no passion to be found playing small–in settling for a life that is less than the one you are capable of living."*

It is possible that you woke up today and realized that your reality is not what you thought it could be and you made the decision to change.

Most of us are given a taste of reality and realize that it is imperative to change our ways for good, but history shows that we have a very short-term memory. We battle through the tough times and then when things start to get better we go right back to our destructive ways. This state of mind is completely temporary because we are faced with reality. You have two choices. Do what you have already been doing with your life, OR decide that enough is enough, it is time to change.

Stop waiting to live the life you want. So many people wait until some arbitrary later time to really live. They wait and wait and wait; by the time they realize their life is over, it is already too late.

You have probably seen the cycle many times already. A person goes to high school, waiting until college to really live. They arrive at college, and then wait until they have a good job to really live. They get that job and wait until they get that promotion or meet that someone special to really live. Then they wait until they retire to really enjoy life, all the while believing that their real life is waiting to start sometime in the future.

Do not live your life like that. It is empty and unfulfilling. Instead, start creating more of the experiences you want for yourself now rather than later. Start enjoying your life, even if it is just in the little things. Start building towards your big dreams. The time to start is not tomorrow, it is now.

As you begin the work of shifting your mindset, make sure you are doing everything necessary to support your new, empowering thoughts. I have found that using positive affirmations on a daily basis will help you stay focused and energized. When using positive affirmations you are essentially speaking to your subconscious mind, actively reprogramming the thoughts that may have lived there for years, but are hindering you from living the life you want. It is important that you create affirmations that are effective for you and your personal situation.

If one or more of the principles in this chapter resonated with you, implement them right away. Do not wait until tomorrow – if there is a single action step you can take right away, take that step now.

While a vague promise to yourself to do something later can easily be forgotten, if you take a powerful action step now, that is something you will never forget. If you want different results, you must take different actions and start living the life you want NOW!

Notes:

ABOUT THE AUTHOR

Dr. Jacqueline Torres

Dr. Jacqueline Torres has over 20 years experience in public speaking and training. She is a nationally accomplished key note speaker, publisher, broadcaster, and voice-over announcer. In addition, she is an author contributing her ideas to the upcoming book *Leadership: Helping Others to Succeed and The Power of Change: Renewing the Spirit of Your Mind.* Dr. Torres is the Chief Executive Officer of Firm Foundation Inc. Firm Foundation, Inc., [FFI] mission is to increase leadership commitment and dedication, creating and developing culturally revealing strategies in programs to help improve the lives of our communities. FFI delivers an interactive and integrated training approach that capitalizes on the expertise and experience of both the participants and the facilitators.

When you encounter Dr. Torres you encounter a person with perseverance and passionate about the work she does in moving you to the realm of exceptionalism and inspirational enthusiasm. She understands that creating meaning and purpose for employees is the key to your organization's success. She has developed thousands of professionals into a better understanding of best-practices in Leadership. Dr. Torres' trainings will leave you in high spirits ready for a commitment and excited to implement the changes whether they are personally, professionally or spiritually.

Amongst other certifications and degrees she is also certified to facilitate leadership trainings and has received many awards on her outstanding leadership work. Dr. Torres will make sure that she works together with the "planning masters" to ensure that the mission, goals and objectives of the organization and its constituents are met at the end of the day. Dr. Torres trusts not just her personal experiences but years of research and investigative work she has done to facilitate the interactive and participatory trainings.

Contact:
Jacqueline Torres, Ph.D.
firmfoundation8@cox.net
860-748-2906
http://home.comcast.net/~firmfoundation8

FOURTEEN

Renewing The Spirit of Your Mind

By Dr. Jacqueline Torres

The programming of your spirit is subject to change. The keyword in the title of this chapter is *Renewing.* In order to empower you from the very beginning and define renewing, I have gone ahead and selected a few choice words. Renewing can mean to modernize, refurbish, repair, restore, mend, remodel, revamp, redecorate, update, revise, amend, modify, adjust, alter, change, improve, correct, rework, transform, convert.

I would encourage you to take any one of these words that will inspire you to heart, the one that you can identify with or connect with the most without loosing focus of the renewing. Do not take it lightly because this is the word that is going to carry you through the thought and change process in renewing the spirit of your mind. I suggest you take that word that you choose, print it in large letters and have it *visible at all times.* Make extra copies to put in your purse, on your car dashboard, your home, in your office, your secret quiet place and so on. You have to mean it, see it, believe it, and be it!

You will be challenged yes, but I believe in you and this is the exciting part of the entire process. If you are not challenged, you will not be motivated and if you are not motivated, you will not be inspired and if you are not inspired, then you would not really understand or know why you are here on the threshold of this new journey in your life. Every chapter in your book of life has different events, places, people, and results. You will realize that you get to choose every one of these elements and who gets to perform, what role to play in the chapter that you are directing and that it will be played out the way you chose. This is the part where you play the main character, get to write your own script and you get to decide the end result of this chapter of your life.

Remember, you have to be willing to start with a clean slate and in order to do this you have to be in unison and harmony with the spirit of your mind and you must have the desire and the will to succeed. You need to know who you are and where you want to go. Create and invent your dream, plan the course of action you are going to take and execute, take by force and bring it to past. In other words, focus on the end result which is your main goal.

Get a pad and write down everything that comes to mind without filtering the thought process. Give your thoughts permission to flow. Your thoughts have power. You create the environment in which you wish to live. You actually create your own world. If you get up every morning and the first thing that you say is, "I hate to get up in the morning," watch what happens the rest of the day. Before you know it, you will encounter or come in contact with people that are feeling the same way and before you know it, you start feeling worse than when you started. That's because you instructed the spirit of your mind in what direction to go on that day and that spirit will lead you to the buddies of that thought because in case you didn't know it, Déjà vu means you might not remember, but your mind does. Yes, that thought knows exactly where to find its roots and its "hang outs" and the end result of that day is hopelessness, despair, sadness and misery. You can't do anything if your whole heart isn't in it because out of the abundance of the heart is how you will perform. Therefore, modify your behavior accordingly because it is wise and to your advantage to ensure that your entire heart, mind, body and spirit is in it—for real!

Now, before we move on, let's stop for a moment. I'm going to walk with you through this journey. Take a deep breath and a moment of silence. If it helps to close your eyes, feel free to do it. Otherwise it's ok to leave them open. Tune out anything and everything, all distractions. This is *the moment*, your moment of reflection. Take your time, don't rush, we're getting ready to make some serious deliberations and decisions in our lives that will make history. Let's quiet our spirit of the mind.

Have you ever wondered what if you had never been born? Take as many deep breaths as you need. This will not only help focus, but also bring transparency, connectedness and give permission to the spirit of your mind to flow. Ask yourself, "What if I had never existed?" Ponder upon this for a moment. Close your eyes and let the spirit of your mind wander. Where does it take you? What does it look like? Who is present? Where is the place? What is the scent like? Consider and deliberate with this for a moment.

I ask you this question because on a certain occasion many years ago, I was in my house. I believe I was doing the laundry and as I was going back and forth into the laundry, a small still voice "the spirit of my mind" said to me, what if you had never existed? I stopped and in my minds eye I looked at those words and immediately started crying, a sense of humbleness came over me and I allowed the spirit of my mind to wander and it took me back to my childhood, my youth and my adulthood years. Through my tears, I started speaking to myself and saying, if I had not existed, I would not have known the people that I know, I would not have traveled the places I've traveled, I would not have known my children, I would not have known my parents or my siblings. What if I had not existed? I would not have accomplished what I have accomplished. No one would've known me or about me. I would not have known or experienced what it would've been like to live in this universe.

It was interesting to me that not once did I think about all the challenges I had in my life, all the sorrows and pain that I went through. Never once did I think about the negative or the conflicts and challenges I had in my life. I immediately went to the positive and the good that had happened in my life. I went to those places that left a positive impression in me, all those things that were significant to me. I suddenly became aware that while the spirit of my mind wandered it made me be aware and observe the purpose and substance of my existence. It was then that I discerned the purpose of my existence and it wasn't really about me, but it was more about them. It was more about the meaning and the implication of the significance of the other people, places and events that came across my path.

It was then that I understood the real reason for my existence. The idea of someone even thinking about me was enough to understand the real reason of my existence. The feeling of knowing that someone felt that it was important that I be part of this world, part of history, part of another person's life was more important than the actual act of existing. That alone was a gift for me to cherish and be mindful of through this life's journey.

The spirit of your mind can take you to your past, your present, and your future, it has no problem traveling and it doesn't need a car, train, bus or an airplane. All it needs is a thought. All it needs is for you to think, to speak and to send it forth.

Being in tune with the spirit of your mind will definitely alter your state of being and will adjust your thought process to the extent that it will bring harmony into the real reason of your existence. It is wise to allow the spirit of your mind to be renewed so that it can refrain from allowing you as a person to think for yourself and bring into the spirit of your mind any chaos, because with the renewing of the spirit of your mind comes a new life, a new beginning, a new way of thinking. No longer will you just do what your mind wants to do but instead you will allow the spirit of your mind to regulate your new way of processing your thoughts. The new spirit of your mind will be paying attention to your new mentality and will "speak its mind" when you try to introduce something of unknown origin that will cause the spirit of your new mind to be offended or to go contrary to its purpose. This renewal of the spirit of your mind will be paying close attention to what comes out of your mouth—if it is for life or if it is for death. The renewed spirit of your mind will disapprove of any negative thinking, but will instead heed to the new way of thinking. Once you have come to agreement that you will start having a new point of view on life and its challenges in a new and positive way. It will probe you, discipline you, watch over you, look after you and care for you as long as you allow it and will heed to that renewing of the spirit of your mind. It will be your responsibility and to your advantage to ensure that you become intimate friends with the renewed spirit of your mind.

It will take some time before you are totally rehabilitated, transformed and changed to the new and improved you, but this course of action and process will require that you be patient and gentle with the development of your new persona. Yes, there are going to be times when you are going to "miss the mark." But that's ok because it is innovative new information, new input downloading into your psyche. Because the renewed spirit of your mind is going to know this, you need to allow the spirit of your mind to get on the same wave length with your new mindset. It is therefore why we need to be careful of what we say. Once the word comes out of your mouth, it will not return "empty handed." It will accomplish that which you sent it out to do—positive or negative.

All the negative that was in the spirit of your mind needs to be replaced or deleted before it can acquire a new transformation in an effort to contribute to the new you. You will have the authority to bring every thought or word against the new you into captivity or control. Whatever you say or do, negative or positive, make sure you validate it. Never end your conversations or your self-talk with a negative statement. Always end in a positive note because you have the authority to change your circumstances. You have not been created with a spirit of fear; you have been created with a spirit of power, love and a sound mind. Your persona plays a role in how you respond to your mind.

You will be in charge of organizing and managing the renewing of the spirit of your mind. Your past does not have to dictate your future.

Your vision of your new you determines your destiny. It is why you cannot be conformed in the old ways but put on the new self which is being renewed in knowledge and wisdom. Remembering to work your goal before your objective. That which was, was, and that which is, is!

With the renewing of the spirit of your mind you will be able to have healthy relationships, positive behavior and an investment in a better future. Remember that you did the best you could with the information that you had and that was taught to you, but now you can change your present and your future with the new tools that have been shared and given to you. You should consider renewing the spirit of your mind every year as if you were renewing a subscription to your new life because you have the power to change! To change your life you have to change the negative message or messages from childhood all the way to your relationships, especially those that were not healthy and kept you bound, bringing them from chaos into order. If Napoleon thought that, *"One must change one's tactics every ten years if one wishes to maintain one's superiority when going to battle,"* how much more often should we as leaders, since we are always in the forefront of transition.

Get the pen and pad, you're on your way to reaching your new potential. You have to imagine in the spirit of your mind what this renewed you looks like. Don't hesitate to think and dream big, take your time, don't short change yourself, aim for the moon, and remember to breathe while writing it down.

Are you ready and willing to change? Are you ready to put off the old you? There are some action steps to this decision. Where you are going you can't bring with you the past or the "old" you because there is no room for both. You can't be double-minded in this new place. Therefore, it is important that the actions you take in this new place is for the betterment of renewing the spirit of your mind. You're developing a new relationship with the new spirit of your mind. Thus, as a mother takes care of a newborn, you have the responsibility and challenge to care, protect, nourish and nurture it! Consequently, you will be able to live a new life by renewing your thoughts and attitude of your mind to the point of maturity and completeness.

Have a phrase ready to guide you and push you to the ultimate goal, which is to have a renewed spirit of your mind. It should be something that will encourage and inspire you to keep on moving to your ultimate goal. For instance, my personal mission statement is I CAN DO IT! For this reason, when weakness tries to show up, I encourage myself by saying this phrase. When a circumstance shows up to discourage, I repeat this to myself, and so throughout the process I am not depending on anyone to encourage me, although if someone comes along and does this it is welcome. But most of the time you find yourself wanting and no one is there to give. That's why you need to remember and learn to encourage, motivate and inspire yourself throughout all the different phases of this new and improved you. After all, most of history has been made with just ordinary people like you and me.

When the spirit of a person controls its mind and its mind controls its body, it is then when that person has learned something about the priorities of life. For that reason, I commend that you put off the old you and put on the new you with a renewed spirit of your mind!

Furthermore, as a reminder, beware of your thinking process which can be hazardous to your health. It's difficult to be all you have been born to be when your inner voice of the past is putting you down. Set some boundaries that will be your "door stoppers" to those hazardous thoughts. The origin of those negative thoughts/attacks comes from areas where you are most vulnerable. When a bad/negative thought comes to mind, say something good/positive to cancel the thought or counterattack. Beware of toxic persons or toxic words because these actions will either be the causes or consequences of what you receive from other people or from yourself. Remember, you are coming from a wounded spirit of your mind to a healing and renewing you. Through it all remember to breathe. Smile, someone cares about you!

ABOUT THE AUTHOR

IRENE C.R. WILLIAMS

Irene Cruz-Ricafort Williams was born in Cebu City, Philippines. Currently residing in San Antonio, Texas, she considers herself fortunate that the innate wanderlust she was born with has simmered down and allowed her and her husband to settle in the Alamo city this last decade. She is a wife, mother of two and grandmother of three. Having found her niche, she credits her eureka moment to her friendship with the Professional Woman Network's founder, Ms. Linda Ellis Eastman, who never forgot even though a lot of time has passed since a small class in December 1993. Ms. Eastman's direction awoke her dormant passion for writing.

Ms. Williams' professional life includes a few years with a quasi-federal government branch; temporary contract work in aircraft manufacturing logistics; directing, marketing and managing a photographic imagery lab, and small retail business ownership. Earlier experience included radio and stage amateur acting.

She dropped out of college and surrendered to the strong desire to see what she could of the world. Her penchant for travel has taken her to British Hong Kong, Tehran, Bombay (now called Mumbai), Bangkok, Tokyo, and London.

She loves to read, favors mystery thrillers and biographies, and keeps her e-reader stocked with her favorite authors. She started writing short stories in Tagalog and English when she was ten years old and discovered she loved writing just as much as acting and singing. Her plans for the future include using her talents to do voice-overs and audio books.

Ms. Williams and her husband both are **cancer survivors** and relish each day. Married twenty-two years, they value the meaning of the vows they said to one another. They look forward to the next two decades! Ardent dog lovers, they have two spoiled rescues that complete the pack: Lucky and Rookie.

PWP co-author projects:

A Journey Within: Self-Discovery for Women – Chapter 12
Living Your Vision and Purpose – Chapter 7
Becoming Your Own Best Friend – Chapter 5
The Self-Architect: Redesigning Your Life – Chapter 11
Bruised But Not Broken -- Chapter 16
Transformation: Reinventing the Woman Within, Chapter 9
Life Is An Attitude!: The Power of Positive Living – Chapter 16
The Power of Change: Reinventing Yourself At Any Age -- Chapter 15

Contact:
(210) 995-6009 • (210) 421-5905
02ireneW21@gmail.com • Website coming soon!

FIFTEEN

The Woman In The Mirror: The Importance of Self-Reflection

By Irene Williams

The Angry Year

Sendi

Weaving slowly out of the fog, she can't figure out why she remembers nothing. She wonders if she will dream. Would a nightmare stay somewhere in her consciousness? She hears strange noises and unnecessary commands. Not sure if they are directed at her, all she can do is peer through the thick wall of uncertainty and open her eyes.

Reality? They have been telling her to open her eyes… Why, so she can go back through the mist and darkness of a drug-induced sleep?

The last thing she remembers before being swallowed by nothingness is his soft voice asking her to 'come back to him.' Did she go anywhere at all? Not knowing if she wants to 'stay' or not, to her surprise, everything seems the same in her world. The only change is the soft echo of his voice, whispering in her ear. She decides to keep his voice in her heart. She still does not want to let go of the heaviness inside. Despite the reality surrounding her, she wants to cling to doubt and sadness. She isn't ready for hope.

Disappointed that she awakens with no memory of any messages from anywhere inside her mind, she tries forcing, daring anything to awaken whatever she must have hidden only to come up empty. 'That anesthesiologist is good,' she thinks; too good.

She feels ugly and she wants everyone to know it. Changing her appearance was an idea that occurred to her when she learned there was no escaping this episode. What statement was she trying to make? She isn't sure, but when people look at her she wants them to see the pain and the ugliness. She wants them to know she is lost and may never find herself again. She does not feel great about herself, about anything. Not now. She has to keep on keeping on. Every day she puts on her 'normal, smiling, business as usual' façade. Her happy self is deep, deep down at the bottom of an ocean full of sadness and uncertainty. On the surface, the life-bearing light is nowhere when she looks up.

She remembers as a little girl, dreaming of sinking, of drowning and being enveloped by murky darkness with no one knowing. Strange that she was always curious about the Sargasso Sea, a lake in the middle of the Atlantic. It is mysterious, deadly and by all accounts so distant, so beyond reach. Now the dream is back, as real as the pain she feels. She only has one choice and no miracles to hold on to. She must surrender to the dream as the creatures slowly come and lead her the way. Slowly treading water, her legs are getting tired and heavy and are about to give up. The more she tries to free herself of the mysterious ocean's pull, the more she wants to give up and give in. Still incensed inside, she is slowly overwhelmed by some kind of peace taking over her sadness and her soul…

Surprising she can still think. Amazing her heart is still beating. How can this be? Wait! Wait! She has not said goodbye. She has never told him how empty her life is when he is nowhere in sight. There is no her without him. After everything they have been through together, she can't not say goodbye.

Miche- Reflections. Regrets?

Espejo mio, fancy meeting you here at this point in my life. It's been a long, long while, hasn't it? I was what, seven or eight years old when I discovered your silence; your enticing, at times, deafening and unbroken silence. You listened intently without judging and accepted my idiosyncrasies, laughed at my blunders. How have I not noticed all these things until now? Perdonar mi ausencia. Forgive my absence. Are you the same friend?

Sendi

In the midst of all the self-pity she chooses to wallow in, a solid portion of sanity tries to peer through. What would she do if she was on the other end of the spectrum? She doesn't know how long her father needed help before he passed. She was told that the 'boys' took care of him. "How well did they take care of him", she wondered.

Would she have taken care of him the way he needed to be cared for? Would he have accepted her help? Would she have had the emotional strength to give him the love she so wanted him to return?

Every once in a blue moon, something triggers the memory of a love story – the kind they both had for each other when she was very young. She recalls how he would get down to her level and tenderly tell her funny stories. She laughed at all his jokes, no matter how many times she heard him tell them.

She was about five years old when her grandmother died. At the cemetery, he knelt down, looked at her and told her that Mama Jul (her grandmother's name was Julia) was gone and no longer coming back. Her heart ached for him. She remembers realizing how different it would be to run up the stairs to Mama Jul's place and not see her beautiful face, her long gray hair… She remembers wanting to be with him all the time and how happy she was every time she heard his voice. That was an eternity ago. Would she have reached deep down inside to retrieve long dormant visages of her adoration for him… and given him what he needed?

Emotionally, her mother left her a long time ago. Still she feels all the pangs of remorse. It was hard for her to define their relationship. To this day, she finds it impossible to think of her mother without id regression. Told that she is a psychologist's challenge and delight, she laughs until she cries. Slowly, surely, she figures out what her mother was all about. But they have already been gone from each other's lives a long while.

Gelba - Something that a Cosmetologist Cannot Fix

One of Robert Louis Stevenson's witticisms talks of some people's hunger for knowledge being such that they swallow the universe like a pill. In their quest, they don't mind making a fool of themselves. One of my closest friends is inarguably one of the muses referred to in this quote. Her name is Gelba. She is Funny with a capital 'F', has a goofy sense of humor, is sometimes out in left field and other times coming from the parking lot! She's careful to keep her goofiness in check. During candid talks, she tells me that all suffering and misery are overrated and that remorse puts deep creases on your forehead that Botox cannot fix. Loneliness, according to her, is what happens when you stay in the shower too long. But really, I asked her what it is about long showers and interminable baths that, according to her, stirs up memories and excavates buried secrets? Gelba's one-word answer: guilt. Guilt has a way of setting your life straight, or askew, depending on how deep-seated it is. Her name was Maria. My friend 'stole' her from her neighbor. Until that time, my friend always considered herself beyond reproach. But people did it all the time. She needed a helper – in other words, a ***maid***, to start her new adventure. It was unbelievably easy. She promised Maria more money, a bi-weekly pay instead of the usual monthly. She entertained guilt pangs briefly and then decided it took two to tango. Maria herself was beyond excited about going with Gelba to a new place, the big city, with the promise of a better life. Well, a different, hopefully better employer anyway.

Transferring to a new college was a big deal. A new boyfriend eased all the uneasiness of a major move. What Gelba did not expect was the boyfriend's reaction. He did not like that the new maid was, to him, aesthetically deficient. He became even more displeased when he found out that Maria's social skills were non-existent. Whenever they had company the poor girl ran to her room and hid. After a couple of months, he insisted that Gelba dismiss Maria and send her home. "Send her home?!" Gelba exclaimed, "After I stole her from my very own neighbor?!" Long story short, Maria was enticed to go home with an extended, overly-generous vacation. When Maria asked my friend when she expected her back to work, Gelba told her to enjoy her trip. Of course, after all the piracy my friend did, the guilt lingered. When she received a letter from Maria wondering when she should return to work, the missive ended up in the trash can.

In an unusually unguarded moment, Gelba asked me if she should have done things differently and how. I gave her my sweetest, non-patronizing smile. Then I told Gelba that, not only did she do the right thing, but that she did the best thing for both herself and Maria. Her face lit up, and we went on our merry way - shopping for shoes.

Miche

How lucky could she be? If she pinched herself every day, someone might tell her its all a dream. No, if it isn't real it would be a nightmare.

His name was Hugh. His friends called him 'Hugo' and she called him 'Russ'. Everyone, including herself, thought how amazingly he resembled the actor Sean Connery except that he was the fairer, blonder version. He was an Irishman who spoke fluent Spanish and hung out with, yes, Spaniards.

He called her his 'buddy girl' when he wasn't calling her Nina. At times it annoyed her that he called her a little girl since she was far from being a little girl – she was eighteen and fully aware she was close to being twenty. She wanted to be twenty; she could not wait to be twenty. Twenty, to her, was the magic number.

Hugh Russell was a contractor hired to do some engineering work by Miche's employer, a pharmaceutical company. She wasn't that curious about his past, and preferred to accept everything he told her about his life in Belfast. The truth was she was afraid to ask since she was afraid she wouldn't know what to do with the answers. They met on a dare. One September night, Miche, her mother and her friends were out celebrating a friend's birthday. They saw him in line to buy jai-alai tickets. The birthday celebrant dared Miche to ask him out on a date. She looked at her mother, who had a big smile on her face, and received a nod. No one was going to call her a chicken. Muttering to herself on the way to making, what she was sure was, the night's, perhaps the week's, most embarrassing event, she cut in line in front of the handsome stranger, aware of the nasty looks the other people in line were giving her.

"My friend, who is nineteen years old today, dared me to ask you out on a date. I'm not sure I am prepared to buy lunch for seven people tomorrow, so if you don't mind, pretend I won this bet by smiling at me and giving me a nod, and I will go back to my seat and leave you be." The look of amusement on his face embarrassed her to no end and she turned around to go back to her seat and admit defeat.

"I will pick you up at seven tomorrow evening at the front entrance so you can show your friends. I will be driving a dark blue car. May I drive you home tonight?" he replied.

Speechless and certain her mouth was open, she finally found her voice and said, "I'm with my mother."

"May I drive you and your mother home tonight? I will need to know where to pick you up in the future, you see."

Miche

Approaching her favorite corner of her bedroom, she sang, purposely out of tune, "Mirror, mirror on the wall… Ola, espejo mio!"

How long has it been since Russ left? It's been quite a few years at least. I feel lucky to have met him, to have spent time with him. It was a different time. The Catholics in Ireland were in turmoil then. Northern Ireland, it seems, will always be in political turmoil. It will never be just about religion.

* * * * * * * * * * * * * * *

The three women whose stories are featured above do not know each other. As far as I am aware, their paths have never crossed. I chose them for this chapter because each one has touched my life in different ways and inspired me. Some of the things they have in common are resilience, each one's ability to survive life's challenges and start over. They are of different generations. This chapter tells of a time in each one's life that caused them to stop, step back, reassess and either start over or continue on to a different path.

Sendi is a teacher and a cancer survivor.

Gelba is an actor.

Miche is an artist. She is an amateur photographer and painter.

Notes:

ABOUT THE AUTHOR

Patricia Villa Avila

Patricia Villa is CEO of MACIE in México City; She is a bilingual Cognitive Coach, Gestalt Psychotherapist, Specialist in Couple therapy and a Team Coach. She conducts seminars and workshops throughout Mexico consist of topics such as "Balance employees = balance company" "Superwoman Reality", "Protagonist or victim which role do you play ", "The art of saying no", "The second adolescence- The Forties", "Who runs my life , better than I do" "Listen to your inner voice".

Mrs. Villa knowledge and professionalism is supported by working with corporations and with humans that are looking for a better and different way to "do" things.

Among her many accomplishments, Mrs. Villa has written several articles for web magazines in Mexico and holds a Business Administration Career with a specialization in Training and Life and Career planning from UDLA College in Mexico.

Articles

- Have we become technology slaves?
- Being "me" being a couple… IS POSSIBLE
- Who really listen nowadays?
- Couple election …Is it a question of expectations?

Certifications

- Certified Gestalt Therapist
- Certified International Professional Coach
- Certified by Ned Herrmann Group
- Certified Human Development Consultant

Professional Spotlight

- Televisa (TV Mexican network) a special blog in their web as a coach and a therapist

Professional Organizations

- The Professional Woman Speakers Bureau
- The Professional Woman Author´s Institute

Contact:
www.macie.com.mx
pva@macie.com.mx
MEXICO CITY
Ph:(52) 555659-8345
(52) 555554-6504
Cell (521) 5518455415

SIXTEEN

A New Attitude! Removing the Negative from Your Life

By Patricia Villa Avila

How easy is it to see a cloudy day and complain about it? But how about a sunny day? How many times do we express, "What a wonderful day"? It is easier for us to see the black spot than the whole picture. Easier or maybe more common because we have been focusing on the black spots that make our life more spotty. Why have we been doing this? Today you have the opportunity to sweep and clean the negativism from your life. I invite you to read the following suggestions that will let you see the whole wonderful picture.

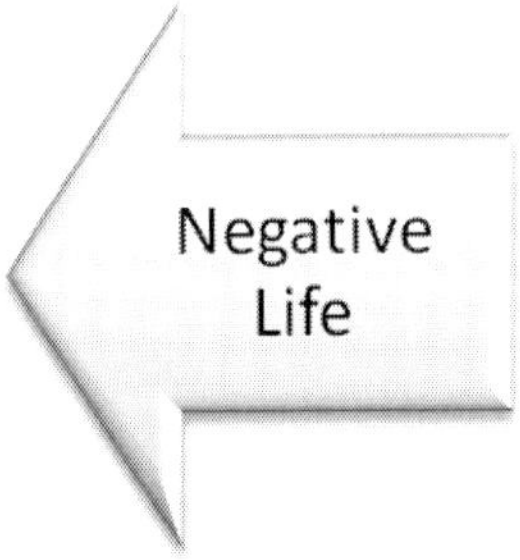

Frustration, bad mood, anger, pain, fear, a gray or black perception of everything and everyone. YOU ARE THE VICTIM THAT SUFFERS!!

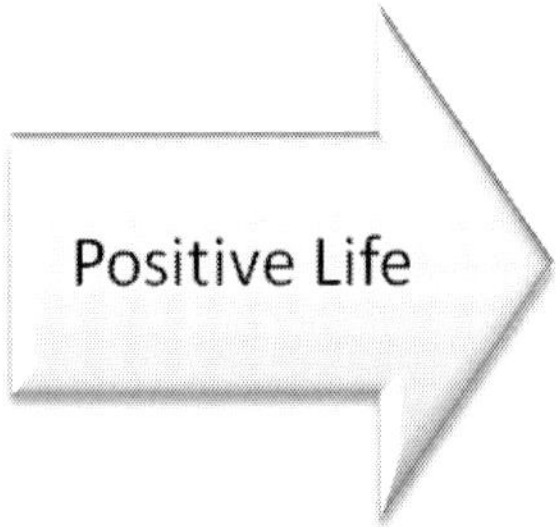

Smiling face, companion satisfaction, wholeness, success, happiness, open to inspiration, forgiveness, peace, YOU ARE THE GOAL!!

Sweep All The Dust

By dust I mean all the polluted words, comments, events, judgments, perceptions, thoughts and ideas that you had allowed to breathe in and carry all these times that created pain, embarrassment, fear and frustration among other things. So, take out your new broom and sweep all this dust. Is your decision to eliminate it or to continue carrying and breathing it?

How Can I Sweep It?

- Think consciously: what do you want to sweep?
- Use your own broom to sweep (If you want to try a difference, use a new broom each time you sweep)
- Don´t forget any difficult corner. You know which corners are really dirty.

- Your ego needs to be swept frequently.
- Sweep all the labels you have stocked, some of them are not yours.
- Forgive the ones that sweep onto you all their dust.
- Forgive yourself for letting yourself carry all that dust.
- Sweep yourself of all the dirt; you don´t need it to be the clean YOU (Unconditioned Self)
- Do not forget to sweep frequently. Make this a habit.

Clean Your Windows

Somebody said that our eyes are the windows of our soul and that means how we see the exterior and the others from our interior. Sometimes, if you have dirt and dust in your windows, it is impossible to see the truth and the reality. So, clean your windows to see the exterior with transparency and reality. Remember, you see things and persons from *how **you** are*, not from *how **they** are*. It depends on perception and everyone has their own perception depending on how they are. When you have a clean window you will see the whole picture instead of bits of things, It will let you have a complete vision that you could turn in to a mission.

Order Your Closet

Acceptance

Abilities

Strengths

Goals

My Reality

If you organize your internal closet, you will start to see what you really want to wear, what really fits you, what is yours or what is borrowed or that somebody gave it to you and you really don´t like it or want to wear it i.e. ideas, comments, judgments, and so on.

Update the ideas, judgments, and comments that you have bought. Some weren't your kind, others are old fashioned and some others are not even yours! Hang onto your experiences as simply experiences; you are not made of them so honor them and commit to the present life and live today´s joy.

Surprise yourself with new outfits (abilities, strengths and talents), redesign new outfits out of some that you like but need to be updated (check your needs, thoughts, and self-concept and actualize it).

Turn The Volume Down

Check the volume of your inner judge. How is it? Is it loud and hard? This inner judge sometimes can be your worst enemy and it is inside you.

To have a positive attitude you will have to put a mute on your inner judge because this judge only perceives you as an "ugly duckling" and will never see the wonderful swan that you really are. So, you have the power to do with the volume button whatever you want; try to MUTE for once! My experience with pushing the mute button on my self-judgment has added a wholeness sensation of my life. Try it! Give yourself a chance and let yourself feel like the beautiful swan you are. Think of it this way:

Loud Judge Volume:

If your judge has a loud volume and is telling you only horrible things to make you feel unsuccessful or like an ugly duckling, YOU WON'T BE ABLE TO FEEL JOY, because you'll block it!

Muting the Judge:

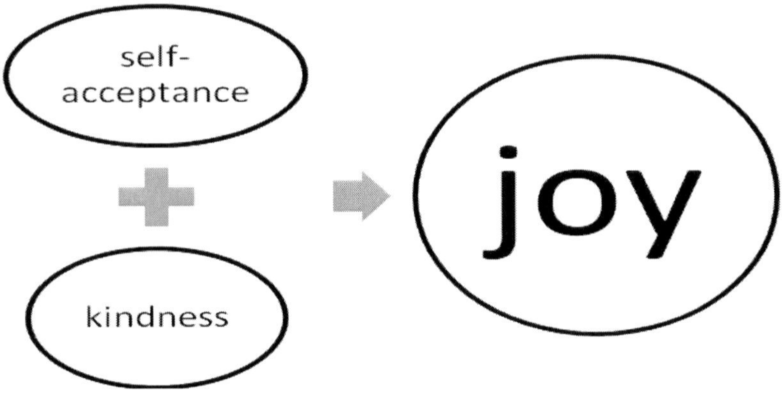

If you mute the judge you will be able to accept yourself just the way you are. If you add to this kindness, YOU WILL BE OPEN TO JOY and this will turn almost everything in to positive ~~and~~ instead of negative judgments! You will be swimming in experience and opportunities which, sooner or later, could bring you INSPIRATION.

Be the Owner of Your Beliefs

Look at this picture, what do you see? Do you see black arrows or do you see white arrows? Your perception of the figure is variable in a way that seems "not to be determined by anything else."

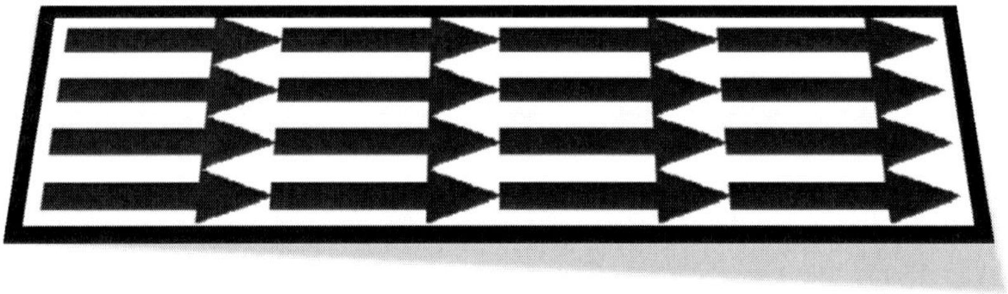

With this picture I want to illustrate how your beliefs have no more power than what you give them! It is up to you to select your beliefs very carefully! The beliefs you have can be transformed by you their owner. Do you want to create joyous and liberating beliefs in your mind? As easy as living in the present moment with only loving thoughts can help to change your relationships, success, job, love and so on, BE AWARE of that bag with harmful and old-fashioned beliefs about your life and start to be in charge and open to new, clear and delightful beliefs. YOU CAN SEE THE FILM OF YOUR LIFE AS YOU WANT TO SEE IT, as a victim or as a protagonist. The choice is yours.

Inspiration on Inhalation

Breathe life and inhale with smiles, hugs, care, motivation, emotive thoughts and all the emotions and sensations that enrich you. In every inhalation feel and stay with the things that give you joy and exhale all of the things that intoxicate your mind, spirit and body as you don´t need to stay with the polluted stuff that only harms and will not let you heal. In other words, take from the outside what you need to be equilibrated and let go what you don´t need to carry in the journey to the positive joy life.

Exercise: Take a really deep breath imagining that you are filling yourself with harmony, acceptance, love and care. Exhale what you don´t need in this moment such as pressure, punishment, judgment and so on. Get it out from inside you. How do you feel after a SELF DETOX?

Shake up your "NO" and put on an assertive "YES." Every time you say YES to something you are saying NO to something else and if it is an assertive YES, it could take you into an affirmative and positive way of life.

Imagine if:

You say NO to saturation in your life and you say YES to space.

You say NO to suffering and you say YES to healing.

You say NO to surrender and you say YES to opportunities.

It is only an example of how we can really transform almost every NO into an assertive YES, now try it:

I say NO to fear, I say YES to ___________________________

I say NO to guilt, I say YES to___________________________

I say NO to loneliness, I say YES to______________________

I say NO to struggle, I say YES to _______________________

I say NO to control, I say YES to_________________________

Your Positive Journal

Every day write down three positive experiences that you had in your personal journal and then write what took you to that positive situation. Over the next year, as you begin to journal you will, in time, have a lot of material to sustain your next life decisions and expectations. Review your journal often and learn from your experiences. This is a positive journal, therefore you are not allowed to write toxic or poisonous sentences or words, not even judgments, which will look like black shadows on it and make it wither. Remember you are writing on a new page which will be filled with your inner positive way of seeing life each day.

TODAY

1. My kids arrive early.

2. I had a wonderful lunch.

3. I enjoyed my workout at the gym.

Commit to Peace

Start by making peace with yourself as this will help you bring peace to everyone else around you. Answer the following questions:

1. Do you disconnect from the NOW frequently?	yes	no
2. Are you to busy "futurizing" or "pasturizing" to enjoy the moment?	yes	no
3. Do you struggle frequently? You can´t flow naturally.	yes	no
4. Are you to busy chasing love, peace, harmony to be peaceful?	yes	no
5. Do you postpone time and room for peace because you are really busy for this luxury?	yes	no

Look at your answers and reflect upon those "YES" answers as these are the little stones in your shoes that do not let you commit to self peace. You have done the first step the awareness. Now, work really hard to transform them into a new attitude of "PEACE", first~~ly~~ with yourself, and allow this to flow naturally with the others in your environment. BE A PEACE MODEL.

When peace is within you:

- Problems become opportunities
- Trust becomes power
- Fear becomes experiences
- Struggle becomes a smooth flow
- Insecurity becomes a commitment
- Forgiveness becomes freedom
- Worry becomes creativity

Focus on Adding

Concentrate all your energy, passion and movements on adding positives to your life. Add a positive attitude about what you think is required to have a great life balance, for example: add creation to the things you enjoy doing and keep on adding whatever you need to be creative.

Imagine for a moment that you are the one who can add many positive, assertive points to your balance. Start to add these to your life. YOU can create this.

What can you add today to your balance? If you find something that will *subtract* energy or passion in your life, then throw it away! Your balance will be focused on adding positives to your life!

Write the things you can add today to your positive life:

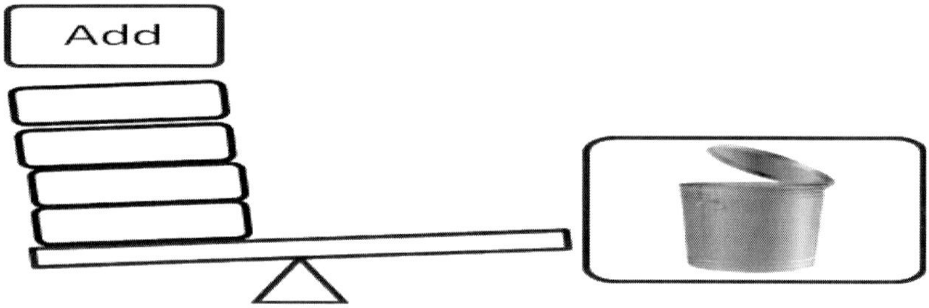

This is a continuing process; you have to practice it in any situation when you feel like going to the dark zone where only the dark spots are seen and not the whole picture. Try to remember the process so it will become a habit and you will remove any dark thoughts, ideas, emotions or even fantasies.

NEW ATTITUDE

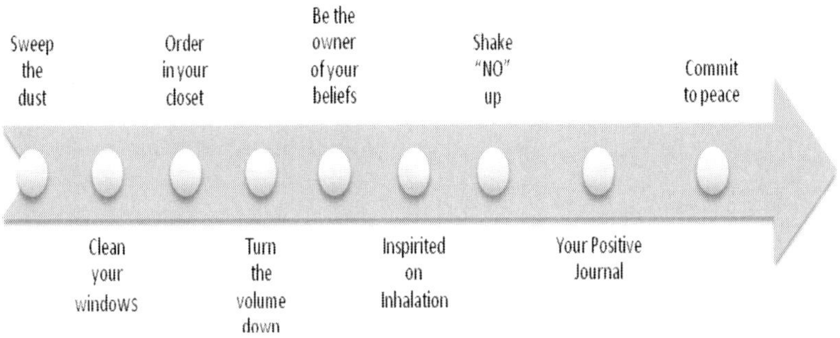

Recommended Reading

29 Gifts: How a Month of Giving can Change your Life by Cami Walker

Now Discover your Strengths by Marcus Buckingham and Donald O. Clifton

Shift Happens! by Robert Holden

Starting Over: Learning to Love Yourself by Linda Ellis Eastman

The Power of Your Subconscious Mind by Joseph Murphy, PH.D., D.D

ABOUT THE AUTHOR

LINDA ROSE MONGELL

Linda Rose Mongell is President and CEO of Marketing Me Ltd., a professional consulting firm focused on enhancing image, brand and culture. She is an accomplished speaker, facilitator, trainer and consultant with more than 25 years in the corporate environment.

Linda Rose has extensive experience and a diverse background in the areas of marketing, executive management, strategic development, retail, public relations and communications, professional development, promotions, sponsorship management, event marketing, new business development, process management and project and event production. She has also designed and developed needs assessments, communication and marketing strategies and various training programs and systems.

Linda Rose holds a B.A. in Public Relations and Communications and is a certified trainer in the areas of diversity, women's issues, brand and image building, as well as a certified coach from the Professional Woman Network. She is an advisory board member of the International Professional Woman Network (PWN), a member of the PWN's Speaker's Bureau, as well as a member of the American Management Association (AMA), American Society for Training and Development (ASTD), and National Association for Female Executives (NAFE).

To add to her list of credentials, Linda Rose is a published author, a recently appointed radio show host, and is also a professional belly dancer and has taught belly dancing for beginners.

Contact:
Marketing Me Ltd.
2913 El Camino Real Suite 812
Tustin, Ca 92782
E-mail: lrmongell@marketingme.com
Website: www.marketingme.com
Office: 714.389.1728

SEVENTEEN

The New You! Reinventing Your Brand and Image

By Linda Rose Mongell

"Think positively about yourself... ask God, who made you, to keep on remaking you."—Norman Vincent Peale

It's time for a new you, or so it seems. The world around you is changing, your life is evolving and every time you look around there is always something new and different. That's life in a nutshell and while you understand that life is taking its course, you've come to a place within yourself that says, "It's time for a new me."

The decision to make some personal changes is far easier to come by for some of us than for others. For some, the decision to reinvent themselves has been prompted by a recent look in the mirror in the fitting room in our once favorite store. The mere fact that "they're not your Mom's jeans" now means you are coming to grips with a personal shortcoming. And let's not forget the inevitable birthday reminder. For some people, life altering events such as a job loss, career change, the death of a loved one, the now empty home or a divorce can catapult us in to making a critical life decision that it's time for a change.

Regardless of what brought you here, any type of change requires work and when we talk about 'Reinventing Your Brand and Image,' we are covering a lot of ground. Because it's about the "real you" we want the world to see and that is reflective in every part of your life. Most importantly, it doesn't matter whether you are a businessperson or not, it doesn't matter how old you are and it doesn't matter where you are in your life to reinvent your brand and image or make the decision to give yourself a bit of an overhaul. Nevertheless, the world is changing around us so we should change, too. We evolve and mature and we should afford ourselves the opportunity to reflect that in who we are and how people see us.

Personal branding is about discovering and communicating your uniqueness. Identifying those qualities that make you who you are and communicating those strengths, abilities and talents which stand out. How and what we express about ourselves is important in all areas of our lives. We should portray our authenticity and be truly genuine.

I believe there is often a misperception about brand and image. A person's brand should never be fabricated or fake mostly because it is deceptive and also because nothing that isn't real has sustainability. At some point down the road the falsity and lack of depth will be revealed and misrepresentation and lack of authenticity is not negotiable.

Each person has his or her own unique gifts. Each person has experiences, history and stories that give each of us meaning. There isn't another person on this planet just like you. You are here for a reason and you do serve a purpose. What you have to offer to the world and others is a gift. How we package and communicate that is an important step in the process. Don't deny yourself the opportunity to reflect on the outside and in everything you do with all of the wonderfulness you have inside.

The truth about who we are individually should emanate from our presence and should resonate from the messages we are communicating. How we look, sound and behave should define who we really are. We need to be true to ourselves, first on the inside and then display it in every way about us possible on the outside. Your brand is you, both personally and professionally. Most of what we read about regarding branding and image is usually in a professional context but branding and image is what matters in a first impression. Whether you believe it or not, we really want to leave positive and memorable impressions on people we meet. I can tell you that, as much as I say I don't care what people think about me, it would be more of a comfort if what they thought was more positive than not. On the other hand, I am honest and comfortable with who I am, with the person I portray and what I believe in and I am willing to express myself in such a manner knowingly accepting the fact that someone may not agree with me or even care, for that matter.

Defining your image and brand is not only about your physical appearance, it is also about the aura that surrounds you. Knowing who you are and what makes you look and feel your best is vital to the image that you portray. If you look at a photograph of someone, what does that photograph speak to? That's an image, the impression you got when looking at the person in the photograph. If someone looked at a photograph of you, what do you think they would say? This is a great exercise if you truly want to re-define your brand. What is the message you are currently sending? If people know you, then based on the experiences and time they've had to get to know you, they will probably say a whole lot more than just what they see in the photograph. We are, however, more interested in what someone who doesn't know you has to say. There is a strong possibility that it may not be exactly what you had anticipated. That's okay though. That's why we can take a fresh start at a new beginning.

The main components of personal image are your attitude, how you communicate, your physical appearance and how you present yourself to the world. These are characteristics that help form a first impression. These are the areas to focus on in order to express your highest potential.

Attitude and Behavior

Attitude shows in your facial expression, your body language, your tone of voice and throughout all of your movements. Confidence is also reflected in how you conduct yourself and how you hold yourself in any given situation. Don't mistake bitchiness for confidence. When you believe in yourself, confidence should be a natural outcome in your posture, the words you say, how you say them and how you control your actions. It is important to be true to who you are because what you are thinking will reflect on the outside, whether you want it to or not. What about negativity? Have you become a complainer? This has serious implications. It takes a toll on those around you and how people perceive you – even your friends. Negativity casts a shadow on your image and it is important to think about.

Communication Skills

Your eye contact, your body movements, posture and hand gestures say more than words. Unconscious hair twirling, picking, scratching, pointing, looking down or covering you mouth are some examples of this. They may show insecurity, insincerity and even contradict what you are saying. You could send confusing or conflicting messages so you won't come across as clearly as you wanted. Think about your posture when you are standing or sitting. Are you hunched over, are you slouching? Is that sending a message? How do you sit down and get up from a chair? Consider your handshake. A strong, confident handshake says a lot about a person. What do your facial gestures say about you? I tend to reveal a lot in my facial expressions. I can tell you I am very aware of it and can't really help myself when I am in situations that prompt certain responses. But, like I said earlier, what you are thinking could likely reveal itself on the outside so, should you happen to be somewhat expressive, I caution you to be prepared.

Choose your words carefully. It's become quite common to hear unnecessary word choices everywhere we go. A "gutter mouth" may help you make a point but does it help you with the image you want to portray? Regardless of the popularity of some key words, using them still denotes a frowned-upon image point.

When we talk about brand and image, one area that we often overlook is our space. Our personal or work space says a lot about who we are. What does yours currently say? Does it define you and say what you want it to say or does it, too, need to fall in line with a need for some tuning? Does grandma's old chair need a face-lift? It is time to part with the chickies and ducks from the 80's or do they still reflect the image and brand you want today? There is always a way to incorporate those things you find important with a newer, fresher look. It's a difficult challenge at times but it's worth considering.

Physical Appearance

The most important component of image is the one you make through what you wear. Your attire, your accessories, your shoes, your hair and grooming, your posture and the overall look of confidence you project are examples of this.

Your clothes should always be neatly presented and should fit properly. They should also be appropriate for your specific body shape. Trends are what they are – trends. This means they come and go and fade over time. Unless the nature of what you do requires you to exhibit the latest trend, I recommend using discretion when applying them to your wardrobe. Classic styles that fit your form are better choices in the long run and carry versatility in various environments than most trends. In the spirit of "reinventing your brand and image" I must mention that "classic styles" from the previous decades such as the 80's or 90's may not necessarily qualify. Just because they still fit, look new, were expensive or you believe they are in style, doesn't necessarily mean that they should be included in this reinvention. This is where I would advise you to either create a partnership with a close and honest friend or consult with a professional image consultant. We have far more options than we have had in the past and a new wardrobe doesn't need to cost a lot of money. Even refreshing our current wardrobe with some new pieces is worth consideration. You must also consider the colors you wear. Now, I know this is not new news. You should wear colors that complement you and enhance your natural complexion. They should make you look healthy and energetic. I am big on color and there are a number of ways to incorporate it into your wardrobe.

Be creative. As for accessories, they should always be considered in small doses. This is actually an easy area where you can adopt a trend if it suits you. Accessories can easily update a look. Handbags should be current and, depending on whether or not it is for business or casual time, a great bag speaks volumes. Again, there is no need to spend a lot of money if it isn't necessary. Your shoes should always be shined or polished. The shoe repair shop should be on your regular circuit of errands. For significantly less than a new pair, they can work wonders with the shoes you have keeping them in great condition.

Don't leave out the basics. Make sure you moisturize. You skin does show through your clothes. Your nails and feet should be manicured and your make-up should always be current. I will say it again; just because you have it doesn't mean you should wear it. If you don't like to wear make-up let me recommend at least a good moisturizer, a bit of blush and lip-gloss. They should be the bare minimum. If you want, you can add a little mascara but never leave home without lip-gloss or lip stick. One more note on physical appearance, if you feel the need to have a little nip-tuck procedure then I would ask that you first do your homework and second make sure it is for all of the right reasons. No procedure is without risk. I live in a very affluent part of Southern California and I've seen a lot of work done on people. Do your due diligence and remember who you are on the inside. Remember, appearances send a message louder than words and create the foundation of your image. Let's make sure we are sending the right message.

Presenting Yourself to the World

Now that we have focused on the basics, let's talk about ways you can present yourself to the world. I believe that nothing replaces human interaction and that the best way to portray your brand and image is in person. We are in an age where so much is happening online that we can't be distracted in such a way that we place more value on being online and involved with our social networking sites than we do in real life-living. Your physical life plays a huge role in your brand and image and should be focus number one. Your virtual life comes second. Regardless, having an effective brand and image requires activity. If you are reinventing your brand and image I encourage you to consider a few of the ideas below. It's easy to talk about attitude, communication styles and physical appearance but now let's really put it to work.

Join In

If you are going to reinvent yourself and if you are in business, consider joining your local chamber of commerce or an association specific to your industry like meetup.com or LeTip. If you can't find one then start one. Even on Twitter, users are starting "Tweetups" where people get together for events. Another emerging concept is that of casual co-working, or more affectionately known as Jelly (workatjelly.com). There are lots of opportunities to develop great relationships with others, especially if you work alone, that can enhance and enforce your brand.

Share What You Can Do

Volunteering is one of the best ways to enhance your brand and image. It sends a message about who you are and the value you have by who you choose to get involved with and help. People don't always understand that the things you do reflect strongly on who you are and that this is all attributed to your brand. Mentor people or teach in your local community. Write books, newsletters or articles.

Write a Professional Bio

Spend time working on or updating your biography. If words don't come naturally or you don't think you have enough information for a biography, have a friend tape record you talking about the things that make you unique. You could also consider a copywriter to write the story for you. Once it is complete, place it to sites like LinkedIn or VisualCV. You may also want to create a portfolio with a book through Blurb. Blurb offers a fabulous online publishing service that, within days, can turn into the perfect portfolio book for you to carry to showcase who you are and what you do.

Education and Training

Pursue your interests. Whether it is for career advancement or personal growth, identify what additional training or education you would like to pursue. It will not only enhance your ability to do a job or provide a service but it will help you stand out and feel good about yourself and the value you add to the world around you. My degree is in Public Relations and Communications but I have never let it stop there. I have a number of certifications that lend credibility and help differentiate me from my competition and build trust. I believe that as long as we are living we should be doing things that help us grown and evolve. In today's business environment, it is especially important to take all the steps you can to maximize the power of your personal brand so that you can stand out from the competition and be ready for the ever-changing market needs.

It's important to establish and maintain both a strong personal and professional online presence. Given the uncertain economic times, you should be actively engaged in how you present yourself to the world (wide web). When people Google your name, what do they find? If it's what you want people to see great, if not then there is some work to be done. Even if you aren't in the business world you most likely are Google-able. If your name appears on a public document or a school you attended you will appear somewhere on-line.

Register Your Own Domain Name

When branding yourself on the web, there's no better place to start than registering your own domain name. If your name is somewhat unique, chances are its available. If you have a more common name, then try lots of variations. Use a domain registrar like GoDaddy or NetworkSolutions to find out what's available. When you've made your selection, buy it for several years at a minimum. Search engines will sometimes take the registration period into account in factoring how valid an address is.

Start a Blog

If you don't already have a personal website, using a blogging platform is a flexible way to make one. To establish a "voice" on the web, create your blog and post observations, thoughts and articles on a regular basis. It is a creative way to express yourself and establish yourself online.

Launch Your Facebook Page, LinkedIn Profile and Tweet

If you don't already have a Facebook Page and a LinkedIn Profile, build your profile carefully using your professional photos and bio. Don't post a whole lot of nothing. Anything you post can help you or hurt you and when information gets on the Internet it lives forever on the Internet. For example, I wrote a press release in 1997 that, if you Google me, will appear somewhere out of the ether. I take social networking sites very seriously and so should you. Unless you don't care about the consequences then heed my advice. If you're already on social networking sites and have embarrassing information, get rid of it. Lose any bad language, revealing photos, blubbering rants and anything else that paints you in a negative light.

Twitter is a service that enables people to send short text messages or "tweets" and its purpose is to learn about news and trends, seek advice and connect with others. I am not a big fan of Twitter but for some it has served some well. So, if you stick with it, Twitter can lead to meeting people where you live or who work in your industry, creating business contacts and uncovering resources.

Reinventing your brand and image can be quite fun. It can also be a lot of hard work. I recommend finding a quiet spot and process these questions:

1. Who is the real you?

2. What are some of the things you can do to make sure the world knows the real you?

3. What are some of the challenges you face in representing your true self?

Then take it one step at a time. We are a work in progress but we should always be looking ahead and never behind. Those days are over and the biggest impact you will have in the world awaits your readiness. Don't miss your opportunity or deny the world your true self.

"We did not change as we grew older;
we just became more clearly ourselves."—Lynn Hall

Notes:

ABOUT THE AUTHOR

Deborah Jones

Deborah Jones was born in El Paso, TX. She has worked for the Federal Government for 34 years with assignments in New Mexico, Texas, Germany, the Marshall Islands, and Virginia.

She has a strong background in leadership roles that was initiated through her experience in both the private and governmental sectors. Those opportunities provided her with extensive organizational and managerial experiences. In addition, years of customer service experience, classroom experience, and public speaking experience has helped her to develop the ability to understand and relate to the needs of the people with whom she works and to present information in a manner that is easily understood.

She has participated in strong leadership programs, such as the True Growth Academy, Leadership El Paso and the USDA Executive Leadership Program, during her career.

She has received several merit awards to include the Superior Civilian Service Award, four Commanders Awards for Civilian Service, and the Achievement Medal for Civilian Service. She has also received honorary awards to include the Honorable Order of Saint Christopher, the Honorable Order of Saint Barbara, and the YMCA REACH (Recognized Achievement) Award.

She is credentialed in International Protocol, Image and Social Etiquette, Event and Meeting Planning, and International Protocol and Business Etiquette. She has also obtained a Business Etiquette Certificate from the University of California, Fresno.

Debbie resides in San Antonio, Texas.

EIGHTEEN

The Importance of Self-Marketing

By Deborah Jones

"Regardless of age, regardless of position, regardless of the position we happen to be in, all of us need to understand the importance of branding. We are the CEO's of our own companies."—Tom Peters

As a woman with 34+ years of experience in the workplace and in volunteer work in professional organizations, I have had the opportunity to observe individuals in the way that they present themselves in the professional world.

I started working in the mid-70's when women were venturing out into the business world intent on making their mark. During that era, there were many challenges to overcome for women to be accepted into the occupational environment as viable members of the working world. Women had to prove themselves capable of accomplishing things that women had not been known to do before, such as running large companies and/or owning their own businesses.

Growing up with parents that always told my siblings and I that we could "be anything you want to be," it was surprising to me that when I entered the workforce, women were still struggling to be accepted as the professionals we are today.

Take, for example, the first female to be accepted into West Point Military Academy. Being admitted to West Point was quite a feat for this young woman and for those who followed in her footsteps. She didn't realize it, but she was a pioneer for future female military leaders. To be accepted into the academy, she had to have exceptional academic grades, had to have an extraordinary military bearing, and had to show that she could compete and succeed in a male dominated environment. I'm sure that being the first woman accepted into the academy was tough on her and that the men did not make it easy for her. Being fortunate to know her, I can attest to the fact that she went on to become an exceptional officer and a high ranking professional retiree. She accomplished this by developing an effective resume, showcasing abilities and skills, and maintaining an appearance that reflected confidence and professionalism.

This example, along with my other observations and experiences over time, shows that it is extremely important for a person to market and/or brand herself to be successful. This sort of branding is a term I will refer to as "self-marketing."

When a person begins to be engaged in "self-marketing," it is essential to include six key areas: (1) creating an elevator speech, (2) providing quality customer service, (3) engaging in continual networking, (4) establishing an appearance that people recognize, (5) establishing an effective phone and e-mail presence, and (6) developing a reputation as an expert in your field. Let's look at each of these key areas in detail.

Elevator Speech

An elevator speech is defined as a short piece of information about yourself that describes who you are and what you are about in just a few moments of time.

As an example, my elevator speech would go something like this. "Hi, I'm Debbie Jones. I work in a field that is equivalent to a corporate event planner for the CEO of a major organization. I plan and execute events attended by affluent civic and military leaders at all levels. Events include ceremonies, dinners, conferences, and concerts, locally, and at times in other areas of the United States and overseas. Activities include determining and securing locations, menus, seating arrangements, audio visual support, contracts, and support personnel."

The elevator speech is a way of utilizing each precious moment of the day to connect and network with key players in the work force. In this "speech," note that I have provided my name, my occupation, a brief description of my job duties, and the location of my work. A lot of information was provided in the time it took the elevator to go from the ground floor to the corporate suite on the top floor, enabling me to sell my professional self to individuals who may be looking for a future employee, colleague, or corporate partner.

Customer Service

Customer service is defined as the means of providing a service to others in a professional manner, in a way that one wishes to have reciprocated, and in a means that makes a person feel valued. As an example, let's look at the difference in two types of services provided to the same customer of an insurance claim. The customer is me.

I moved from Virginia to Texas in 2005. Since I was new to Texas, I had to change my car insurance and drivers license within 30 days of becoming a citizen of that state. I met with a couple of insurance agents and one of the agents impressed me; let's call him Agent A. Agent A was a caring individual that made it known he was interested in his customers needs. His caring ways made it evident that I could call on him with questions or concerns, knowing I would receive prompt customer service either from him or from his assistant.

A couple of years later, I received a letter that Agent A was no longer with the agency and that my policy had been transferred to Agent B. My new agent, Agent B, sent me a postcard stating that he would be handling my policy from that date forward, but never made an effort to contact me or to meet me in person.

I was a victim of a hit and run auto accident prior to Christmas that year. I tried to contact Agent B to let him know that there had been an accident and that I was not injured. When I called, I received his voicemail and left a message, but Agent B never called me back. I know that telephone etiquette has changed over the years, but I was surprised that he never returned my call. Since I never received a return call, I had to go through the "central" line of my insurance company to report my claim. I was very disappointed with the lack of "customer service" I received from Agent B. I was so disappointed, in fact, that I contacted my insurance agency and told them that I wanted a new agent.

Providing effective customer service only takes a moment. A brief call, a short email, or a quick note in the snail mail is all it would have taken to feel that I was important and my needs were important. Agent A made me feel valued and Agent B made me feel unvalued.

If Agent B had been my customer and I had received a message that there had been an accident, my first action would have been to contact him, inquire how he was doing, ask if he or any family member had received any injuries, and find out what I could do for him in filing his claim, in finding an auto repair shop, etc.

In all businesses, strengths and weaknesses come across in everyday interactions. Agent B, through his lack of customer focus, lost a customer. It is important to remember that every phone call, e-mail, and note (or lack thereof) sends a message of who we are, what we are about, and what makes us tick. Caring and positive customer service markets us in a manner that will be eternally remembered and makes us notable in our fields of service.

Networking

Networking is defined as a means of making personal and professional connections with other individuals within the job market.

As an example, when I first entered the workforce, I worked for a woman who would attend every luncheon, every reception, and every social event hosted by the office, civic organizations, etc., whether or not she knew any of the people present.

She was an expert at self-promotion ("self-marketing"). She would speak to everyone in attendance, volunteer to give talks and presentations about leadership roles, and hand out her business cards at every opportunity.

She became active in and spoke at professional organizations. She realized that if she wanted to become known and perceived as successful, that personal relationships and connections were crucial.

By speaking at community groups and by hosting seminars, she became known as a trusted advisor and made a positive name for herself in the community and in the workplace. She made a "brand" for herself as a professional woman and leader. She built her reputation in a positive manner and people began to seek her out for her expertise. She consistently made connections and built a network of people. By putting herself in professional networking situations, she established a large client base.

In every networking situation, I noted that she was always aware of her appearance. She dressed professionally, always made eye contact with the people with whom she was conversing, displayed exceptional communication skills both verbally and non-verbally, and continually handed out her business cards to the people with whom she came in contact. She established why she was valuable to people, showed that she could provide a service, and exhibited that she should be sought out as the professional expert in her field.

I learned a great deal from this individual and have, since that time, always tried to emulate her personal style and communication skills. I learned that networking allows a person the opportunity to make those personal and professional connections that enables women to break the glass ceiling.

Appearance

For the sake of this article, appearance is defined as the overall look a person projects to others at a given point in time; to include attire, eye contact, stature, facial expression, etc.

We all know people judge one another within the first six seconds of meeting. We also know that even though first impressions are superficial, they have an immediate impact on the person making the observation. People immediately notice things such as race, gender, dress, weight, height, hair color, etc. Right or wrong, people instantly make assumptions about others, even before anyone exchanges a greeting. Those instant assumptions are the main reason why everyone should always be aware of her professional appearance and why she should dress appropriately for the type of profession she represents. A person should always be aware of the image they are projecting to others.

An individual's professional image depends a great deal on the type of business in which she participates, the culture of the organization, the geographic location, and the personal contacts within the work setting.

As an example, I've had the opportunity to live and work in several different locations both within the United States and abroad. These experiences have given me the opportunity to observe others and to note what is considered acceptable work attire in different parts of the world.

I grew up in the Southwest, where work attire is somewhat casual. Men commonly wore the guayabera (often referred to as wedding) shirts. These shirts were made of cotton and were worn as a means of coping with hot weather. They were acceptable work attire, as they were somewhat stylish, although at the same time, casual and lightweight. It was also very common to see men and women wear cowboy boots. Men wore their boots with their business suits and women were often seen wearing them with skirts and slacks. It wasn't until the movie "The Urban Cowboy" came out that I realized that this was not common practice elsewhere.

I later moved to Germany and the area I lived in was cold year round. I realized very quickly that wearing leather soled shoes was not advisable or safe. Everyone wore "tread" on their feet so they could safely trek to work on the snow and ice. Many of the Americans wore their treaded shoes to work and traded for more stylish fashions until the end of the day and traded back for the journey home. Purses and handbags were also replaced with backpacks so that more clothing (i.e. fleece, sweatshirts) could be carried around.

I then moved to the Marshall Islands where "common" work attire were shorts, t-shirts, and flip flops. As no cars were allowed on the island, everyone rode bicycles to work, so everyone also owned a "rain suit" – a plastic suit that covered you from head to toe to keep you dry in the rain. Because of the job responsibilities, I wore long dresses almost daily; I never wore hosiery and always wore casual sandals. "Island Formal" was a Hawaiian shirt and slacks and was only worn on special occasions.

Before moving back to Texas, I lived in Virginia where work attire was much more formal. Virginia has four seasons, so dress for each season changed. Business suits, shoes (i.e. pumps, boots, etc), and hosiery are everyday attire on the East Coast. I personally prefer this type of dress because it presents the wearer in a much more professional light.

Obviously, where you live, where you work, the type of business profession you are in (artist versus banker versus carpenter, etc.) should determine your style of dress. Adding your personal touches assists you in standing out from others. The best piece of advice a self-marketer can provide regarding professional attire is an old piece of advice – "Dress for the job you want, not for the job you have."

Phone and Email Presence

Phone and email presence is defined as the professional means by which one quickly responds to the needs of someone on the receiving end of a phone call or email response.

A phone call or email message should be handled quickly, effectively, and professionally at all times. A caller should always be made to feel that she is important through the professional presence of the self-marketer. A self-marketing professional always projects an interest in the calling or emailing party, an interest in providing prompt feedback of the information requested, and an interest in following-up on the thoroughness of anticipated outcomes.

As an example, in my job I am on the phone quite often during the day, providing information or answering questions. I'm relied upon to be knowledgeable about the topics of conversation and it is up to me to provide the required information. If I can't answer the question, I let the person on the other end know that I will do my best to find the answer and will promptly call them back when I have the information. I ensure that I follow through with these phone calls before the end of each work day. People always remember those who follow-through to be helpful. It also permits the calling party to be aware of how important she is to you and your business.

A self-marketer knows phone messages should be short, friendly, and courteous. A self-marketer also smiles when talking on the phone because, believe it or not, her smile comes across on the other end of the phone line as being friendly and willing to help.

Another example is the use of email. The use of email is extremely valuable to self-marketing. The contents, the tone, and quickness of a response all reflect on the professionalism of the sender. I use e-mail consistently in my work environment and receive over 50 emails per day and probably send out just as many. It is one of the best ways to communicate with people all over the world and to quickly receive needed answers to questions and concerns and to obtain information required for everyday work situations. Maintaining email records is also a good way to prove that required work has been accomplished.

Just like with the phone call, an individual should ensure that all emails are professional in nature. A person should proof read and spell check every email before it is sent out. Even when someone does something that projects you or your organization in an unprofessional light, a self-marketer always responds professionally. If the email responder is upset, she should wait until she is calm to respond. If she responds professionally, she will always be seen as a professional.

The manner in which a person responds to both email messages and phone calls reflects on her personally and on the organization in which she works. Therefore, an individual should market herself in this arena the same way she would market herself in a face-to-face situation.

Expertise

Expertise, for our purposes, is defined as an area of specialty in a certain subject matter or job responsibility.

Developing an area of expertise is invaluable to self-marketing. It enables a person to talk about a particular subject with confidence, to serve as the go-to person on the subject, and to be viewed as one person who is able to assist in that respective area.

As I mentioned in my elevator speech, I serve in a role similar to an event planner for a CEO. In this role, I am seen as a subject matter specialist, the go-to person, the person that other individuals can turn to when they need information or assistance. To develop this reputation, I always try to look for assignments and projects that showcase my special abilities. I seek creative ways to put forward my special skills. I want the right people to recognize my potential for upward movement and growth. It is imperative to cultivate a reputation of doing things well, doing them on time, and providing first class service.

Every person has a special skill, talent, and/or an area of knowledge that no one else possesses. The self-marketer finds ways to showcase these characteristics by volunteering to do things for others, by publicizing her accomplishments, by sharing her knowledge, and by demonstrating she is confident, valued, and needed in the organization.

In summary, self-marketing is invaluable to everyone seeking to enter, move forward in, or to lead in the job market. Self-marketing is especially important to women because even though there have been advances in what was previously a male-dominant arena, women must still sell their skill, productivity, and expertise to other professionals. By creating an elevator speech, providing quality customer service, engaging in continual networking, establishing an appearance that people recognize, establishing an effective phone and email presence, and developing a reputation as an expert in your field, women will continue to shatter that glass ceiling.

As for me, although I try to live by all of the above standards, I try to live mostly by my favorite quote by Dr. Seuss. *"Be who you are and say what you feel because those who mind don't matter and those that matter don't mind."*

Recommended Reading:

The Brand You 50 : Or : Fifty Ways to Transform Yourself from an 'Employee' into a Brand That Shouts Distinction, Commitment, and Passion! by Tom Peters

ABOUT THE AUTHOR

EUGENIA HARRIS COOLEY

Eugenia Harris Cooley is a member of the Professional Woman Network (PWN) and co-author of Reinventing Yourself at Any Age. She is presently teaching 3rd grade at Hurden Looker School in Hillside, New Jersey which she describes as one of the loves of her life. She is driven by her love of children and passion to motivate them to succeed in live. She has over fifteen years of experience in the areas of Customer Service and Sales. She holds a Bachelor's degree in Marketing from Kean University in Union and a Master's degree in Education from St. Peter's College in Jersey City, where she graduated with honors. Ms. Cooley is a member of Bethel AME Church in Vauxhall, New Jersey Education Association, Alpha Delta Kappa Sorority (International Honorary Organization for Women Educators), and the International Reading Association. She believes that if you put God first and family second, everything else will properly fall into place. Her favorite scripture – Philippians 4:13, "I can do all things through Christ who strengthens me". She is the mother of two lovely and talented daughters; Danielle and Alyssa-Symone.

Contact
(908-463-7620)
gco27@comcast.net

NINETEEN

Life After Loss

By Eugenia Cooley

Do you ever find yourself asking, "How did I get here?" What began as a perfect and normal life suddenly turned upside down. It seems like everything that is clear and familiar to us can become anonymous and estranged with the blink of an eye. Overnight, nothing tastes or smells the same. Within seconds it can all be erased.

For me, it began with an early morning phone call. As usual, I was running late for work and when I heard the phone ring I was about to ignore it as I would normally do. Not because I was trying to beat the clock but because I was too self-absorbed to do so. I was employed by the local telephone company as a Customer Service Representative. I was tied to a phone daily from 8 a.m. to 6 p.m. most days listening to the grumblings of those that would not or could not pay their bills, others that wanted new service or to move service at what they felt should be a moment's notice, and a few that just wanted to talk just because there was life on the other end of the line. Did I mention this was a stressful position? (High paying but, stressful nonetheless). Basically, I loved the money but hated the job and when I returned home I completely ignored my home phone. Yes, it annoyed me totally and so did anyone who had the nerve to call me as I prepared for work, or to take my girls to school, or even church. I also was not fond of cold weather, winter, and anything related to either. Thus, on this very early December morning, when I heard the phone ring I was not pleased. I am not sure what made me back track toward the phone but I turned back and proceeded to answer it. Oh, I was ready to give the brave soul an earful. On the other end of the receiver, I found my aunt. She sounded anxious and said that she had just received a call from the hospital regarding my mother. "They called me because I was listed as the emergency contact," she spilled out. She then added, "They said she is not doing well and want someone to come to the hospital." Okay, the self-absorbed, spoiled, only daughter of two children that wanted to run away from what did not sound good at all said, "Well, I am on my way to work and I am late." I did not really want to say it or even care about the job. I suddenly felt panic like I had never felt before. My aunt, the oldest of my mom's four living sisters was not letting me off the hook that easily. She simply said, "I'll meet you at the hospital," and hung up. I froze! I could not think, move or speak. I was afraid of my thoughts and revelations rushing through my mind. They were telling me that my mother was gone and that the hospital could not say it over the phone. Another voice (my denial) was telling me that if I just ignored my aunt and went on with my day then none of this could be possible. Then more thoughts and voices put their two cents in the pot. They were reminding me that I never picked up the "sugar free mints" my mom asked me to pick up for the patient in her adjoining hospital room. Imagine that, she is in the hospital (for weeks) and worries about some else. She worried when the other patient did not have visitors or family. She worried if they were ignored by hospital staff. She was always putting others before herself and she had selfish me as an only daughter.

I am not sure exactly how long I drove around before I decided to make my way to the hospital. I can recall lots of procrastination as fear took over my thoughts. Once I arrived at the hospital I realized I did not have any cash on me and there was no parking on the street. I thought, "When I get upstairs Mom will probably have a couple of dollars stashed somewhere." – so I entered the parking garage. As I closed the car door, I froze again – "She is gone, I feel it." Now the bargaining with God begins. Only He can fix this situation. I will walk slower and talk more to Him. I told Him I was sorry for not getting the "sugar free mints" she told me to get. I even promised to go straight to the store as soon as I leave work and pick them up if He spared her. Then I remembered our conversation the night before. It was incomplete. "That's it!" When the conversation ended, it was interrupted by a visitor and she said, "I'll talk to you tomorrow." My mother would never let me down and break her word. Now I walked with a confidence. I do not know what my aunt thought was going on and I do not know what the hospital felt was so necessary to disrupt our lives so early in the morning, but I was on my way to check on my mother and then proceed to work. As I stepped off the elevator, something was off again. God, please rearrange this situation; I am not buying into this. I approach the nurses' station, something is off again. Why are they looking so solemn? God please rearranged this situation; I am not buying into this. There is my aunt standing in the hallway and it appears that her son is supporting her. Now it is all her fault! "Why is she approaching me in tears?" She is ruining everything. It has all been worked out with God and now she is destroying it. "Stop crying!" I scream in my head. I felt that if this behavior continued, then there was no turning back. "Why is she buying into this?"

The Loss

"She's gone!" was all my aunt could get out amidst her sobs. I was completely confused, pain-stricken, absorbed with fear, and immediately felt alone. This was very new, this feeling called alone. I had to see for myself. Maybe there was a mistake. I went into the room and nothing could have prepared me for what came next. It has been exactly 11 years, 2 months, and 3 days since I walked into that room and saw my Mommy lying there cold, stiff, and alone. I suddenly felt a disconnect from life. There was no replacement for Mommy. There was no one that could understand my pain, the true person I missed, and that could guide me as I continued to develop as a mother.

That disconnect and self-pity remained with me for several years. It accompanied me as I lost my job, where I had been for more than decade. It held my hand as I lost relationships. It cleared a path as I gave way to a depression deeper than the Grand Canyon. It was my closest friend as I consumed prescription meds to pacify me. It stripped me of everything I enjoyed in life. Springs and summers came and retreated, my beautiful daughters were managing without me, my father was managing without me, and my relationship with God was totally estranged. This pattern continued for many years until I began to hear God's voice again and see His movement in my life.

The Life After

I began to hear God's whispers. They were not clearly recognized, but He was calling me to reclaim my place on Earth. He spoke to me through my daughters when they would fill the house with laughter. Even though I was resistant to mentioning or hearing my mother's name, it was God that allowed my daughter's to retain the memory of their precious grandmother and keep it alive in their stories. They spoke of her daily, defying my objections. My youngest, which was just shy of five years of age when my mother left, would ask to buy flowers and visit her gravesite at those special occasions. These actions were bringing me back to my position on Earth. God finally directed me to rejoin the workforce. It was a very difficult time; our economy had completely changed during my absence from the world around me. While I had more than ten years of Customer Service expertise, a Marketing degree and a mountain of talents – there were no jobs available. Temporary Agencies were even facing a downward spiral. I began to wonder if God really meant for me to return to the workforce.

Time to Reinvent Myself.

God directed me to obtain certification to become a substitute teacher. I was sure He only meant for me to do this on a part time basis until the economy picked up. After contacting several local school districts, the one that seemed interested in me was the one of my parents' hometown. Upon completing my first day's assignment, I realized God's plan for me. I stopped questioning Him and continued to follow His lead. He led me and kept me for two years as a substitute teacher, the second year even with benefits. The following year He encouraged me to pursue courses, get my teaching certification, and opened a full-time teaching position for me. To further prove that He was not through with me, He led me to enter and complete a Master's program in Education within 18 months. All of this while my oldest daughter was beginning college. God was constantly sending messages along the way to let me know He was with me. His primary message to me was that life does go on after loss. He kept saying it was okay to walk on unfamiliar territory. Through the hidden blessing He was bringing me closer to my mother. He brought me to her hometown, but more importantly He was bringing me to a place that was near and dear to her heart – HELPING CHILDREN. Once I realized that God had a purpose for my life, I was able to move forward with His perfect plan.

What Has Been Your Experience With Loss?

By definition, loss means the act of losing a possession, according to the Merriam-Webster dictionary. In reality, this can be anything from the loss of a loved one, loss of a job, divorce, an empty nest situation, and the list goes on. The bottom line is that loss is personal and when it knocks on your door there is no way around answering. You must keep in mind that no matter what comes your way, God can and will bring you through it all. Psalm 30:5 tells us, "His anger lasts for a moment, but His favor lasts a lifetime: Weeping may go on all night, but joy comes with the morning." Will there be pain at times? YES. Will it hurt and be difficult to face? YES. Will God be there to wrap His loving arms around you in the end? YES.

Put It On Paper.

Take a moment to make a list of your experience with loss. Divide a sheet of paper into three columns. In the first column, list the painful loss (or losses) you have experienced. In the second column, describe what the experience was like for you and what you went through. In the final column, describe the outcome and how you survived it all. If you are still in the midst of your personal storm, then write your prayer for outcome in the final column. No matter what stage you find yourself currently in – SEEK GOD'S WISDOM. My painful experience lasted years because I was not focused on God, but His favor was there for me all the while. You may find yourself in a dark place like a tunnel, but God's light is there at the end. All you have to do is walk toward His light!

Never Underestimate God's Potential in You.

You have many hidden talents and gifts from God that are waiting to be unveiled. How many times have you said, "I would love to do that" or "I wish I could do that?" Stop second guessing God and what He has given you. This may be God's way of encouraging you to move toward your passion or the gift He has already given you. You have already suffered through a loss, now it is time to heal. What better way to do this than by immersing yourself in the reinventing of yourself! In 2 Corinthians 5:17 we are taught, "Therefore if any man be in Christ, he is a new creature: old things are passed away; behold, all things are made new." I once read an article about a woman who was a successful author and cooking show host. What surprised me was when she described her previous life. It was pretty ordinary and somewhat dark. However, throughout her personal storm she always loved to cook, even when funds and food were low in supply. Cooking was her gift and she allowed God to guide her to be reinvented.

What Gifts Are You Suppressing?

Take a moment to uncover your gift and take the first steps toward your reinvention. The following steps will help you develop a plan and set it in motion. Rome was not built in a day, but it was not built without a plan. What do you have to lose?

Step 1 – Make of list of the things you enjoy doing most of all.

1. ______________________________

2. ______________________________

3. ______________________________

4. ______________________________

5. ______________________________

Step 2 – Describe how you feel when you are engaged in these activities.

1. ______________________________

2. ______________________________

3. ______________________________

4. ______________________________

5. ______________________________

Step 3 – Describe how you would feel if you could do this daily and be paid to do so.

____

____

____

____

Can you see the light? Can you see what God's plan for you may be?

Step 4 – Make a list of professional opportunities, careers, or home-based business that involve these activities.

1. ______________________________

2. ______________________________

3. ______________________________

4. ______________________________

5. ______________________________

Step 5 – Do the research! Find your dream opportunity. There are many websites and books available to help you with the search. This can be taken on as a part time project or lead to a full time career.

Be blessed and be anew!

ABOUT THE AUTHOR

TALISA BEASLEY

A sought after speaker, certified life coach, author and consultant, Talisa Beasley is the founder of In the Beginning Consulting, a full service empowerment firm that serves as an educational and personal development consulting firm committed to strengthening families by empowering women and youth. Ms. Beasley is known as the "Benefits Coach" who seeks to help her clients become aware and increase their benefits so that their dreams move from fantasy to reality. She conducts workshops and seminars throughout the United States and abroad. She is best known for her contagious spirit and passionate delivery in her contact with her clients. She is a master at helping to facilitate change and goal achievement in the lives of her coaching clients, audiences and workshop participants.

An expert on Women's Issues, Ms. Beasley is a certified life and executive coach who has served hundreds of clients throughout the United States. Ms. Beasley is an active member of the American Association of Marriage and Family Therapists, Professional Women's Network, Professional Women's Speaker's Bureau, and The Atlanta Women's Network. She has received numerous nominations for awards and been selected by Metropolitan Who's Who as the New and Upcoming Professional.

A supporter of empowerment in body, soul, and spirit, Ms. Beasley is available to consult and keynote on a national and international basis.

Contact
In The Beginning Consulting
P.O. Box 48332
Atlanta, GA 30362
(404) 849-7544
Talisa@inthebeginningconsulting.com

TWENTY

Embracing Change and Transition

By Talisa Beasley

"Change is the essence of life. Be willing to surrender what you are for what you could become." —Author Unknown

A young mother is cooking dinner for her and her three children. She has worked all day and feels her muscles screaming for her to rest. But she must press on and get things prepared for her family. She has had a hard day at work and at the end of the day, her boss informs her that she needs to come and see her first thing in the morning. She ponders what the boss may want. Her thoughts drift as she considers what she may have done wrong to deserve this. Why is the boss picking on her? As she continues along this thought pattern, she wonders how this may affect her or her family.

Does this person sound familiar to you? Have you ever had to go through a difficult moment like this? The truth is, many of us have had to struggle with the thought of how things change rapidly within our lives. While we are going along great, change comes to serve notice that she has never left and can strike at any moment. Currently, a recession has caused our country to be in an uproar about the major changes it has had to endure. Change is the topic of many of the major news networks, and on the mouths of most in this world. The question is how to deal with change without falling apart. Does change come to harm you or to help you? How do successful people handle change? These are some of the questions that we will explore in order to develop the answer that best serves us.

Personally, change has always been present in my life. I will admit that I was not good at accepting change, but I am learning every day to work my way through it. I will have to say it was the words of an elder in my community that helped me to understand how to deal with change. She said to me, "The world is not all about you and the quicker you embrace this, the easier it would be." Now, I know this doesn't sound like much, but I was going through a traumatic moment in my life, and my feeling was no one cared about how I felt. However, once I heard the words of this elder, I began to see things through the proper lens. It is through this lens that I want to place our focus.

How do some handle change better than others? One of the answers to this question is to understand that some of us welcome change, while others seemed to have the "deer in headlights look" when change comes around. The Webster's Dictionary describes change as a process of exchange or to interchange. By definition, the dictionary explains that change is a *process*. This means that you do not remain still but continue to move. Let's use the word navigate. Through navigation, you are going towards a specific destiny. I feel that most of us struggle to understand this idea when change shows up. This is the reason for most of the fear that is experienced, mainly because we don't know where we will end up. This is the place for our "aha" moment! I say this because I want to point out that you are in charge of where you end up. Change is only the *process* or the mechanism for getting there! So the bigger question is where do you want to go? Once you have figured it out, you are happy to see change show up. This means that you move closer to the destination of choice. Isn't that great?! Now let's get our navigating glasses on and focus on how to get to your place called "there!"

There are three components of change:

1. Accept
2. Adjust
3. Align

Accept

In today's world, acceptance is a hard pill for many to swallow. It means that if you accept, you agree. Even if you don't agree, you have to accept. This is often associated with negative situations or negative people. But let's shift our focus to what is positive. Have you ever noticed that when you accept something, the stress is your body decreases? When you say to yourself, "I resolve within myself that I will accept this," your body immediately moves back to a mode of equilibrium. It seems that your body is waiting on your permission to return to a place of rest. The same happens when you accept change. Make up your mind that you will see only the good aspects of accepting change. An example in today's world is the way people have to learn to cut back and avoid excessive spending. More commercials are popping up on television that promote positive characteristics in people in order to promote positive thinking, and to help people move away from the negative effects of the recession. Studies have shown that positive television helps to lighten the hearts of those who watch. Just the other day I saw a commercial about a young boy who wandered onto a stage of a well known pianist before his concert. Just before the show, his parents were frantic because neither one of them could locate the child. Both began to blame the other. All of a sudden, the young boy showed up on stage playing a little tune on the piano! They were so embarrassed that they slouched down into their chairs hoping to avoid being seen. Meanwhile, on comes the pianist who walked up behind the boy only to encourage him to continue to play as he also played the piano with him. The parents quickly noticed how the pianist welcomed the boy and helped him to play even better. (Did you see that shift?) After the little tune was finished, the pianist praised the boy by telling him he had done a good job. Of course, everyone applauded. Notice how things changed when the pianist made light of the situation by playing with the boy. By changing his view of the situation, the boy got a private lesson with a well known pianist, and his parents were proud of their son for his accomplishments. This can happen for you! Examine your situations and identify how it can work for you. Accept the changes that come in your life! Accept that you are getting older! Oh wait, that's negative. Accept the gray hair and remember that it represents wisdom. Accept the fact that your kids are leaving for college. You now have more space to make that room a place of relaxation. Accept that you will have to go to college to advance in your job. Keep in mind that going to college benefits you first, then your company. The key is to remember that as you move to a new area, you direct the navigation system! The only question left is to determine where you are going. That is completely up to you!

Adjust

Pearl Bailey once said, "You must change in order to survive." Most people do not look at change as a matter survival. However, change requires movement. Have you ever seen people who refuse to change? They look aloof and out of touch. Imagine the person who refuses to shop in the store for their food. Instead, they want to hunt and grow their own vegetables. Although noble, they look a little silly. Consider the person who struggles at exploring new technology. Can you imagine your mother who refuses to change her rotary phone? When challenged with changing, she explains that there is nothing wrong with her phone. Silly, isn't it? Well, this is what happens with many of us when we refuse to move along with the change. If we examine the reason for our refusal, we often find that changing means that we have to admit that we may not have the best answer. Rather than admit it, we hang on for dear life hoping change will just give up and let us win.

Let's switch focus to see the benefits of adjusting. Can you remember the last time you bought a new piece of technology? (Ok, this is probably recent!) Let's say you were going to buy a new flat screen television. You were so excited knowing that you were going to the store to purchase it today! Once you got it home and figured out how to work it, you sat and watched it for hours. You called a friend and talked about your recent purchase. You talked about how helpful it was and what additional actions it could help you to accomplish. Sometimes your joy was so contagious that you convinced your friend to also purchase the item. Did you notice that the focus was not on how long it took to read the manual in order for the television to work properly? All the focus was on purchasing and watching the television. This is how adjusting affects people. In the process of gaining new opportunities and skills adjustment is required. This is your bonus on the journey toward "there."

Here is the key to positively adjusting: Keep the end goal in mind! This is a key area that many forget in the process of change. Due to the difficulties that may be encountered in the process of change, people tend to get lost in the struggles. Remember that struggles or problems are only in place to help you to grow and learn. Growth may produce some pains from the process of moving to a different level. This is why the end result should always be in the forefront of your mind.

Let's look at some examples. Child stars are often the subject matter for the "Where are They Now" shows that examine what has happened to them in their search for fame. Many stars are witnessed falling down under the weight of adjusting to the demands of being taken seriously for their talent in their craft. However, the ones who achieve their goals are often given much more acclaim. They are interviewed on what it took for them to make it. One of the main responses is that they remained grounded and kept a strong support system close to them. When I have had the time to catch some television, I have seen how some child stars have successfully identified that they needed to make up their minds to never stop moving toward their goal. This is the attitude that must be adopted in order to understand the process of adjusting. 2 Timothy 4:7 says, "I have fought the good fight, I have finished the race, I have kept the faith!" This passage suggests that the writer knew that there would be struggles, but finishing the race was always the focus. So, let's switch gears from fighting adjustment and make up your mind to get the prize!

Align

Have you ever driven a car that seemed to drift either to the left or right when you are driving it? Mechanics say that the alignment needs to be adjusted in order for the car to drive more smoothly. Automobile websites state that the purpose of aligning your tires is to avoid wearing down the tread and having a smoother ride in the process. If alignment is not handled, the damage could go as far as the steering column and even further damage to the vehicle. This concept is synonymous with our lives as we want to avoid further damage to our life.

The final component of change *requires* alignment to the process. Did you notice the emphasis on "requires?" It can be unfortunate if we miss this as change continues to move in spite of your lack of cooperation. Since we have been discussing cars, have you ever noticed what happens when two people are riding a motorcycle and they hit a turn? One leans with the bike while the other leans away from the curve. This will cause the driver to wreck. The reason for this is that both riders of the motorcycle must decide to move with the bike. They must work in unison. You *must* work in unison with change. Fighting it will only cause you further pain. Webster's Dictionary defines alignment as the support of an idea. By this time, you have been supporting the idea and moving along with the change. However, it has gotten hard this last part of the journey and you are considering not moving with the change. It is at this time encouragement is the most beneficial. You must encourage yourself to complete the task. Donald Lawrence's song, *Encourage Yourself* talks about this very thing.

The song states at times you will have to encourage yourself even when others are not around. I am told that the hardest part of any journey is the last part. But I am also told that those who endure to the end are given a special prize. I encourage you to FINISH! Let's examine how to make that possible.

Those who struggled through the changes within our country during the Civil Rights Era I classify as a special group of people. When they are interviewed, they discuss the struggles and the hardships they endured. They have born the hate and tolerated ridicule for their beliefs. But what stands out the most to me is the determined look on their faces when they sensed victories. They endured being jailed, being beaten, and even death. However, retreating was not an option! Recently, a well known congressman was honored with receiving the highest honor for a civilian, The Medal of Honor. When he was interviewed, he told of the struggles he endured, but he emphasized how he *aligned* himself to the dream of freedom. He commented about his thoughts of the possibility of not living to see the freedom he fought so hard to obtain. However, he stated that this never made him waver in his actions, and how happy he was to be honored to receive a medal for his efforts in the fight. Are you seeking the freedom that change can offer you? Are you aligning yourself with the vision of the change? Are you in it for the "long haul?" Are you able to withstand in the midst of struggle and fear? As we have discussed earlier, change requires you to catch the vision and endure to the end.

There is one final point about alignment. If you are going to align yourself with something, make sure you keep your eyes open for the benefit. Alignment allots for you to benefit from the partnership. This is also true in business partnerships. Many partnerships are developed for the sole purpose of gaining a benefit. In some cases, it is a merger to help improve business. This should be the same for you. If change is coming and demanding you to align with it, then examine the change and determine what the benefit will be for you! For some of us it is accepting where we are in life. For others it may be accepting the next step in our lives. In all of this there is a benefit to be discovered. If I am facing retirement, then I welcome the opportunity to place more focus on myself and enjoy my time off work. If I am facing a change in my finances, then I am to benefit by simplifying my life and avoiding excessiveness. Overall, there should be a benefit involved for you.

Through our discussions about change we have discovered that change comes without serving notice of its appearance. However, we have explored the benefits that change has to offer. I would encourage you to remember that change has a lot to offer you. All you need to do is provide the direction for the change. Earlier we brought up the question about how successful people embrace change. The answer to the question is that successful people welcome change because it creates opportunities to increase knowledge. Yes, change brings about new ways and new opportunities to obtain knowledge. The truth is, when things stay the same newness has no opportunity to present itself. As human beings, we are ever changing. As a result, we should welcome change. However, we live in a society that does not embrace us as we age, so we grab onto products that stop that process. But the reality is that we are maturing daily. The key is to embrace this concept. Have you ever seen a person that looks good at a particular age? The reason is that they have embraced the changes in their bodies and learned to master the direction. You can do this too!

Believe me, change will benefit you in every aspect of your life! Recognize that things change for your benefit and the benefit of others. As mentioned earlier, change is essential for life! So, I challenge you to go after that job and leave fear standing at the door! Transition into school with the contagious vigor of knowing that you will be a success in anything that you encounter! Step back into the driver's seat and tell change that you are driving the car and you can dictate where you are going. Maximize every opportunity by regaining the energy, passion and intensity in your life through the embracing of change and transition! By knowing that you can become whatever you can see, change will come into agreement and create the path for you to get there!

Blessings to You!

Notes:

ABOUT THE AUTHOR

Robin West Smith, PMP

Robin West Smith is a native Detroiter and is a product of the Detroit Public School System. Robin earned several credits toward an Associate's Degree from Wayne County Community College District (WCCCD), but was never able to complete it. After two decades of child rearing, she decided to transfer her credits from WCCCD to Wayne State University (WSU) and completed her Bachelor's Degree in Economics, a Masters in Urban Planning with a concentration in Metropolitan Growth Management and a Certificate in Economic Development. She is now pursuing a PhD in Sociology at WSU. Robin is a Certified Project Management Professional (PMP) with the International Project Management Institute, a certification she completed while pursuing her undergraduate studies at WSU, and a certified trainer with the Professional Women Network in Kentucky.

Robin is currently contracted to teach Project Management courses for ESI International. She completed a brief assignment as a Deputy Director for a non-profit focusing on commercial and industrial businesses on the eastside of Detroit. This opportunity helped her tremendously with a hands-on approach geared towards her graduate studies. Her previous employment in the Information Technology arena with EDS and Strategic Staffing Solutions allowed her to develop a diverse background in dealing with multiple executive levels in corporate America. As a Technical Consultant, she has been inspired to look beyond her comfort zone and prepare to venture out on her own.

Robin is conscientious and organized which has helped her in every venture she has undertaken. Her latest venture is founding Jazmine's Corner (named after her oldest granddaughter), which will be a workshop series geared toward advising middle and high school students on project management, college preparation and other issues pertaining to youth. With these traits, Robin embraces challenges as opportunities for growth. She strives routinely for professionalism and excellence and puts maximum effort into every task she performs. Her civic commitments have included being a member of the NAACP, the Project Management Institute, the Detroit Entrepreneurial Institute, Association of Business Women (ABWA), Women of Virtue Development Institute and the Wayne State Alumnus. She has spoken at numerous Boys & Girls Club Career Day events for various Detroit middle and high schools.

Contact:
WADE Training and Consulting Services, LLC
3430 East Jefferson, Suite #741
Detroit, MI 48207
(313) 657-4616
Westsmith57@sbcglobal.net
www.wadetcs.org
www.robinwestsmith.com

TWENTY-ONE

Overcoming The Empty Nest Syndrome

By Robin West Smith

"A Mother is nothing without her children."
—Marty's mother from the movie, Marty, 1955

As I begin this chapter, I am home alone and contemplating life as an *empty nester.* Our youngest daughter will be twenty-two in June of this year. I recently pulled out her photo album and looked at the pictures of her, beginning with the first ultrasound picture, to the first birthday pictures. Looking at all of the pictures over the years, I wondered as many of us have wondered, where did the years go? No matter how many children you have in life, the last one is the one that really forces you to look at life and ask yourself, *Am I ready to go it alone?* After all, if you think about my opening phrase, ***"A Mother is***

nothing without her children," you wonder, are you really nothing without your children? Well, relax, you are still something when they are grown and gone, but you must be prepared to cultivate that life style BEFORE they leave and not wait until after they are GONE! This is where the real work starts.

The opening phrase of this chapter was taken from a movie made over 50 years ago when attitudes about children were very different. Many children stayed in the home with their parents until marriage, which meant they were well past the adult age. But as time changed, so did children's attitudes about home life and when to leave the security of Mom and Dad. Today, most children leave for college with the intent of never returning home again. However, due to current economic times, many children do return home after college. Regardless of the financial conditions, at some point in time a parent must prepare their mindset for the day when the house will be devoid of children and life must go on.

Although parents tend to experience what I like to call *separation anxiety*, mothers and fathers experience this syndrome very differently. This chapter will delve further into this and by the end of the chapter, not only will the reader have a better understanding of this syndrome, but it is also my hope that the reader will have a better understanding of themselves. There are some good things about this situation that might not be visible to the naked eye. For example, when was the last time you could walk through your house in your birthday suit without having to worry about the children coming home? Can you remember the last time you put something in the refrigerator and found it there the next morning? Not to mention, fewer loads of laundry to wash.

Defining Separation Anxiety

Defining *separation anxiety* is the first step to overcoming the empty nest syndrome. You have to *understand* before you can *accept* what is happening to you. Webster's II New Riverside Dictionary defines *separation* as "a place, line or point of division" and *anxiety* as "a state of uneasiness: worry; fear that lacks a specific cause." When you combine the two words, one might say that *separation anxiety* is "*a state of uneasiness caused by the division of a place, line or point*" in life. Another way of looking at this is to say that when the reality starts to sink in that one has come to the end of their child rearing years, they may begin to start acting a little weird. In actuality, they are beginning to experience the *uneasiness* of what life will be like now that the children are grown.

I am not a trained clinical psychologist, but I do hope to become a trained sociologist in the not to distance future. Sociologists understand the development of human society and why society behaves as it does in given situations. I am a professionally trained Certified Project Manager, and as such, have had to deal with *separation anxiety* with project team members. A project is defined as a "temporary endeavor undertaken to create a unique product, service or result" (PMBOK Guide: 34). Raising a child is analogous to delivering a project's unique product. Project managers work with project teams to deliver successful project results, just as parents work together to raise a successful child. When the project is completed, a good project manager will help its team members transition out of the project. It is at this point that many project team members begin to experience *separation anxiety*.

The ability for any human being to separate themselves from anything is difficult enough, but for a parent to separate themselves from one's child is probably one of the most difficult life experience of all. In the next few sections of this chapter I will go into more detail on a mother's perspective, those who don't know how to let go versus those who do (what do they know that the rest of us don't), my own personal experiences and how I hope to prepare the reader for this inevitable life transforming experience. As I mentioned earlier, it is much better to begin this process **BEFORE** the kids are preparing to leave home, rather than **AFTER** they leave. Begin to *invest in yourself* now. As stated in the AARP March/April 2011 issue, "An empty nest doesn't have to equal an empty life."

A Mother's Perspective – We Have The Cord

Kori Rodley Irons is a blogger for *www.families.com* and writes that "Attachment and separation are one of the ongoing struggles of the parent-child relationship. I am of the opinion it is one of the most intense, amazing, joyful and painful relationship bonds and attachment/detachment dances we are called upon to do in our entire lives. We often talk about young children experiencing "separation anxiety" when they are forced to be apart from their parents. But, I think that we parents experience plenty of separation anxiety too." Because the female is blessed with carrying the child in her womb for at least nine months, when the *umbilical cord* is cut at the birth of the child, it is the mother who first experiences this anxiety and has to deal with letting go of that child.

As a mother who has been blessed to give natural birth to two beautiful daughters and marrying a man and gaining two more children in that process, I have literally had to deal with *separation anxiety* from two very distinct levels. The first level was with the sharing of the child rearing of my step-children and then sending them back to their mother after the weekend ended or when we came back home from the family trip. Having the oldest three children, who were separated by two years each, in the home and then giving birth to our last child was the scenario I had dreamed of all my life. For whatever reason, I always wanted four children to raise, and by the grace of God, my dream had come true. It wasn't easy building a bond with my step-children, but it was well worth the anguish and pain to forge the relationship of mothering with them, as well as with my own two children.

As I mentioned earlier, having the oldest children just two years apart (12, 10, and 8 when we had our last child), it didn't take long for those six years to pass and we witnessed the oldest daughter graduating from high school. What a difference four years made with their development. When I witnessed the eldest daughter walking across the stage, some twenty years to the day when I made the same walk, I began to understand my own mother's joy and tears of watching me graduate. Although our oldest daughter did not leave for college, we did have to accept that she was leaving the nest to begin her new life as a mother. Now she is preparing to watch that daughter leave for college this year.

Dealing With Separation Anxiety – A Personal Experience

The next level of dealing with *separation anxiety* came when it was time for the second oldest daughter (who is actually my first born daughter) to leave for college. This experience was by far the most devastating on many accords. First, Jenifer and I had been a duet for almost a decade when I married my husband. We had a very close relationship as most single mothers and only children would have. I hadn't even seen a R-rated movie during those years of child-rearing.

She was my only priority and everything I did was for her. She was eighteen months old when I decided that she needed to start attending daycare (prior to that she had been with a private home sitter). I had found a wonderful church not far from my home that had a reputable establishment. I was advised that she would have to wear a uniform to daycare and would be able to start immediately.

We went and purchased the uniform. It was the cutest Scottish plaid jumper you'd ever seen with the matching white blouse and red tights. We got up early that morning for the first day of school. I dressed her in her uniform and before I knew it, there I was, crying like a baby. It was at that very moment that I realized this event signaled that the next few years would be like a dream in the night. You go to sleep and they are your little darlings that you hold close to you at night; you wake up in the morning, and they are leaving you forever to begin their life. She asked me why I was crying so hard and I just looked at her and said, "Mommy is just so proud of you!" She smiled and we walked out of the house. When we arrive at the church, I bent down to kiss her goodbye and she held my face and said, "Don't worry, I'll be fine. You have a good day at work, Mommy." She was always very mature for her age.

The years did go by very quickly and the day had come to send her off to college. We couldn't afford to buy two plane tickets so it was up to her to make this trip alone. We were fortunate to find a great deal on an airline that was offering a round-trip ticket for $99.00 over the Labor Day holiday. This gave her the option of coming back home if she wanted to. Being the young lady that she was, I knew she was going to stay. We agreed that I would just walk her to the door of the airport, but I broke that agreement as soon as we got to the airport. I made up some excuse about needing to make sure she could get past security with the laptop computer that I had given her for school.

We made it through the security checkpoint and were well on our way to the departing gate. To set the stage for you, it was about 6:30AM at one of the country's largest, busiest airports on a Friday morning. We had to wait a few minutes before she could board the plane and all was well until they announced that it was boarding time. All of a sudden, it was as if someone had just cut my stomach open and poured a ten-gallon pale of water into my system. The tears came rolling out of nowhere and I fell to the floor of the airport. She quickly grabbed me and pulled me up and hugged me. There she was, the little girl that I took to daycare having to comfort me instead of it being the other way around. She asked me to stop crying because people were looking and thinking that I might need medical attention. As I watched her walk through the gate, I knew I had done all I could as a parent and the time had come to trust her to make the right decisions from this point on. I waited a year to visit her at college. I needed that time to accept this new stage in my life.

She completed her college degree one year ahead of schedule and was ready to return home. But deep in her heart, she knew that she really did not want to come back home. She wanted to move forward with her life. She met a young man while away at school who happened to be from West Michigan and decided that she would move to his city and they would become a couple. She found a great job and things were going well. They found a nice apartment in the city and it looked like they were going to make a go of it. When they announced that they were getting engaged, I was a little skeptical. After all, was he going to take care of my little girl like I did? Once again, I had to accept that she was capable of making an intelligent decision and would have to trust her. They married and were quite happy until the economy took a turn for the worse and he lost his job. Relocation to another state became the only available option.

The day came for them to leave. By this time, they had had a child. I had the pleasure of being her childcare provider for her first year. When we met at their house to say our goodbyes, the lady who had dressed her daughter for her first day at daycare suddenly appeared out of nowhere. Once again, it was the child comforting the parent. I knew in my heart that this time there was no coming back. She was grown, married and a mother. It was time for her to assume the role I had prepared her for and would have to feel confident in my parenting that I had done the best for her.

When it is Time for the Last (or Only) Child to Leave?

For many of you reading this chapter, the last child may well be the only child. The experience of dealing with an only child leaving the nest can be more difficult. You have not had the prior experience of mothers who have had multiple children and who have prepared themselves for this inevitable moment. You may find this time in your life very discomforting and extremely painful. Feeling sorry for yourself is not an option. You have survived the most challenging opportunity ever presented to you when you have raised children. Let this be the *second* beginning of your wonderful life. I suggest the following tips for getting through this period:

- Accept that you have done the best for your child.

- Do not attempt this transition process alone; Find a friend or a support group.

- Volunteer with a childcare center if you need to be around children.
- Pursue one of those passions that you put on hold.
- Go back to school and finish that degree you had to put off.
- Get a part-time job and treat yourself to a new wardrobe.
- Do something, but don't just sit around feeling sorry for yourself.
- If you are single, start dating again.
- If you are married, start dating your spouse again

My point is that these days will seem very empty unless you find new ways of filling them with activity that focuses on you. Going back to the point I made in the opening paragraph, start thinking about the life you want to cultivate when it's time for that last (or only) child to leave home **BEFORE** they leave and not **AFTER** they leave. It cannot be overstated that being a parent can be one of the most rewarding and difficult times in our life. As mothers, we have many challenges to face and obstacles to overcome during the childrearing years. However, always remember that unless you develop a major illness, you have a great deal of life left in you when the children have left home. The final section of this chapter will focus on mothers who chose to *live* the life that is left and those who chose to hang on to their adult children and *lose* the life that they have left.

Mothers Who Don't Know How to Let Go vs. Mothers Who Do

When I opened this chapter, I referenced a movie from 1955 that was titled, *Marty*. I highly recommend you find this movie and watch it alone. It focuses around a man named *Marty* (played by Ernest Bourgnine), who was from a large, Italian family that lived in a relatively nice flat in the Bronx of New York. Given the time period for this movie, it wasn't uncommon for adult children to live at home with their mothers. All of his siblings had moved out, and *Marty* was left with ensuring that his mother was continuingly provided for because his father was deceased. Yet, it was always his mother that insisted it was time for him to meet a nice girl and get married. *Marty* was quickly approaching his 40th birthday and was in agreement with his mother that it was time for him to do just that. By the same token, he was also worried about his mother and how she would fair if he did take a wife and move out.

Marty's mother had a sister who was in somewhat of a similar situation and her only choice was to move in with her son, his wife and their child. She was always complaining about this arrangement and it became unbearable for her daughter-in-law, so *Marty's* cousin asked him if his mother could move in with them. *Marty's* mother thought it was a great idea and, of course, being the dutiful son that he was, agreed to the new arrangement. The plan was set for her to move when, as to be expected, she had a complaint about the new arrangement. *Marty's* aunt is the best example of *a mother who does not know how to let go.* In one scene of the movie, the aunt cautioned her sister (*Marty's mother*) on the possibility that if *Marty* ever married, that her sister could easily become the next victim of relocation. After all, daughter-in-laws are known for wanting their husbands all to themselves and not having their mother-in-law around to muddy the waters.

It was during that conversation in the scene that she uttered the words, *"A mother is nothing without her children."* You have to consider the context in which these words were stated. It was a different time then and women had very, very few choices about their life after child rearing. This is no longer the case in present day. We have many, many choices about life after child rearing. Yet, in spite of the variety we have in life, there are still women (and I don't mean just older women, but younger ones as well) who have trapped themselves into their children's lives and believe that they have no identity without their children. One might understand this if the women allowing this to happen to them are single mothers, but, this is also very prevalent among married women. When the children leave home, many marriages end in divorce because the couple forgot how to have a conversation that did not include the children and their daily needs.

Letting go is a *process*. Webster's II New Riverside Dictionary defines *process* as "1. A series of steps or operations toward a desired result or product. 2. A natural action or function marked by gradual change from one state to another." Understanding that a *process* takes time, overcoming the empty nest syndrome is a process that will take the parents time to adjust. After all, you spent the better part of a quarter of a century child rearing. This was the major facet of your life and when that result is completed, it can leave a large gap in your daily routine. I mentioned in the last section that if you are single, start dating again; if you are married, start dating again. I suggest this in all sincerity. According to AARP, "It's true. Sex can get better after the kids move out." (Saltz & McLeod: 70).

The AARP article continues, "When kids leave home, the parent more involved in caring for them often loses part of his or her identity. As a result, partners may find each other dull…An empty nest doesn't have to equal an empty life. If you see this time as an opportunity, your relationship—and your sex life—can thrive." It can be difficult for couples to navigate this part of their life together. Research has shown that when the children leave home, this change can trigger divorce in many couples because they believe that they have little left in common beyond parenthood. According to a study conducted in 2008 by *Psychological Science,* women actually experience an increase in marital satisfaction after the children leave home. The AARP article suggests the following for couples struggling with this situation:

- Remember where it all started.
- Make allowances.
- Embrace the difference.
- Stoke the flames.
- Invest in yourself.

Parents who are able to let go of their children are those who understand and accept the completed process. This does not mean that your relationship with your children end, it simply means that it moves to another state of being. It is quite enjoyable to have a relationship with a grown child as it was when they were young. But it is also important to remember this is not the time to develop a relationship with your child that could be construed as a friendship. I have witnessed many parents who believe that after their child is grown, they can now become best friends. Be a friend to your children, but always remember that you are their parents first and foremost.

Moms, Don't Forget Dad – He May Be Crying Inside, Too.

I chose to devote this last section to the fathers. Women are capable of releasing their emotions without fear of shame and ridicule. Men, on the other hand, cannot always process deep emotions. I have witnessed my husband "patrol the house" when our daughter does come home at the time he expects her to. I have witnessed him arguing with her over insignificant issues because he simply cannot accept that her days living at home with us are numbered. She is attending a local university and in the interest of expenses, is able to remain at home with us. Yet, as she comes close to completing her studies, she realizes that her career opportunities are going to be best served by relocating to another state.

Unfortunately, the burden falls on our shoulders to help them through this process. He will become difficult to live with, because as men, it is their job to protect the family. It may become necessary to seek professional support if you are concerned that your mate is having problems adjusting to life without the children in the home. Communication is extremely important during this transition. It is not important to win the arguments during this rebuilding period, but it is very important to listen to the complaints. Many of them will have nothing to do with the issue at hand, but more to do with the absent child. This can be even more prevalent in homes with an only child. The attachment between a father and his child is often underestimated. They are already a little jealous that we had the cord, so make every effort to help him feel that it's okay to cry. But never let him forget that he did his best, also.

Recommended Reading:

http://parenting.families.com/blog/parents-get-separation-anxiety-too

Gail Saltz, M.D., McLeod, K., AARP The Magazine, March/April 2011

Notes:

ABOUT THE AUTHOR

Stacy L. Page

Stacy L. Page is a skilled professional with seventeen years experience in Criminal Justice, Legal, Education, and Management industries. She is a personal and professional coach, educator, speaker, mentor and entrepreneur. Stacy's passion is to equip individuals with spiritual and psychological tools that will assist them in navigating the pathways of life and achieve the highest level of personal success. Her mission in life is to empower, motivate and inspire others to fulfill their unique purpose in life.

Stacy holds a Bachelor of Science degree in Criminal Justice from Sam Houston State University and a Paralegal Certificate from Southeastern Paralegal Institute. She also holds Master of Arts degrees in Organizational Management from the University of Phoenix and Clinical Psychology from Argosy University. Stacy is currently pursuing a Doctor of Psychology (Psy.D.) degree in Clinical Psychology at Argosy University.

Stacy is a certified Girls Empowerment Coach and Federal Grant Reviewer. She is a member of the Professional Woman Network, American Psychological Association and the Texas Psychological Association. She is active in church ministry, volunteers in the community, and serves on non-profit Boards of Directors.

Stacy is the owner of Serenity Insight, and provides professional coaching, education and consulting services. Her expertise areas include character, leadership, management, personal and professional development. She also focuses on self-esteem, self-identity and girls and women's empowerment. Stacy is available for coaching, seminars, workshops, consulting and speaking engagements.

Contact:
Stacy Page
Dallas, TX
Phone: 214.215.4729
Email: spage@serenityinsight.com
Website: www.serenityinsight.com

TWENTY-TWO

Change Your Mind, Change Your Destiny

By Stacy L. Page

"Your mind is a powerful force that holds the insight, tools and resources that lead to fulfillment of your destiny."—Stacy L. Page

YOU CAN CHANGE YOUR DESTINY IF YOU CHANGE YOUR MIND! Every woman was uniquely designed and created for a special life purpose that only she can achieve and accomplish. That means you have a designer destiny that no one else on this Earth can carry out except you. You have been given the wisdom, knowledge, talent, skills and abilities that will help you complete your life assignment. The pathway that leads to your purpose in life begins with your mentality, which is your mental power. Thus, it is important for you to have a mindset that focuses on those things that will empower you and propel you towards your divine destiny.

Your mind is a very valuable and powerful tool that shapes your mentality, and it determines your thoughts, emotions and behaviors. When you think about your mind, it is the vessel that contains your mentality, which influences your attitude and outlook on life. If you possess a healthy mentality, then you will have a positive attitude towards life. You will expect, seek and experience the best that life has to offer. If you possess an unhealthy mentality, then you will have a negative attitude towards life. You will not seek and expect good things to happen in your life. Possessing a positive mindset will help you create a bigger, better and brighter future!

Your mentality, or mindset, is directly connected to your destiny and ultimately leads to your divine purpose in life. Changing your destiny begins with changing your mind, and you can learn to change the way that you think. You should focus on changing your mentality by identifying, evaluating and modifying your thoughts. Transforming your mindset will help you focus on fulfilling your destiny and living a meaningful life. It is critical and imperative that you transform your mind and fill your conscience with thoughts that are healthy and positive. God tells us in the Bible to, "Be transformed by the renewing of our minds." (Romans 12:2). Each day we must fill our minds with thoughts that will empower us to approach life with faith, hope, belief and optimism. We must also cast out any thoughts that will cause us to become fearful, hopeless, doubtful and discouraged. Therefore, transforming your mind and reprogramming your thoughts will help you make decisions that will determine your destiny.

There is a mind and destiny connection and you may be wondering how this is so. Your thoughts related to your destiny are first conceptualized in your mind. Essentially, what you conceive in your mind and believe in your heart, you can achieve. Speak this statement out loud to yourself, "**MY MIND CONCEIVES IT**, **MY HEART BELIEVES IT**, and **I WILL ACHIEVE IT!**" Your underlying core beliefs influence your thinking, and cognitions guide your emotions and behavior. Thus, your thoughts subsequently determine how you feel and how you act. Possessing a positive mentality leads to healthy thinking and allows your feelings and actions to align, which will ultimately lead you on a path to fulfill your life purpose and reach your divine destiny. The following diagram is an example of how core beliefs and thoughts influence emotions and behavior.

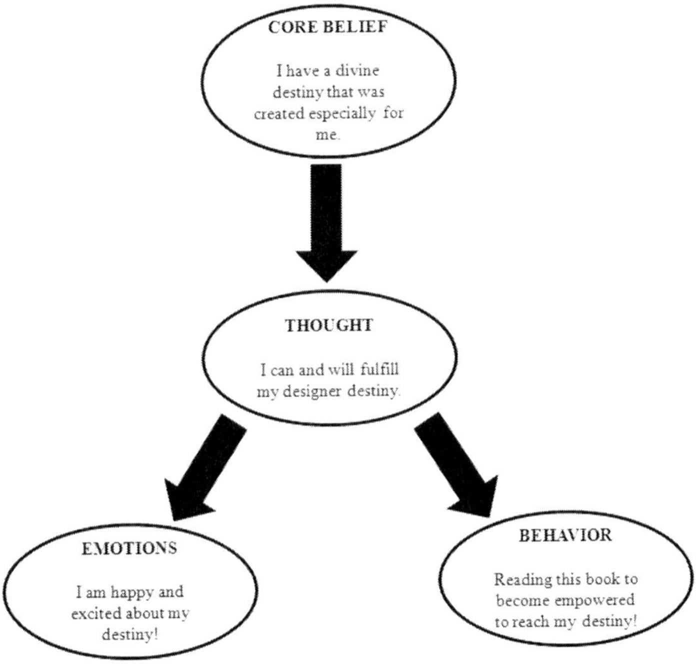

Connection between Core Beliefs, Thoughts, Emotions and Behavior Planting the Seeds

Think of your mind as a garden where you plant seeds that will take root, grow strong and blossom into beautiful flowers. The seeds represent your core beliefs, and they should be planted in fertile soil. After the seeds are planted, you should nourish and water them daily so they can spring forth from the ground. The flowers that ultimately emerge in the garden are your positive thoughts, or cognitions, which serve to guide your subsequent feelings and actions. When you think more positively, your subsequent emotions and behavior will be affected. Positive thoughts will motivate, inspire, and encourage you to walk in your destiny. Thinking positively also gives you hope that you can and will fulfill your purpose in life. Positive thoughts will help you face adversity and overcome any obstacles that may block your path. Healthy thinking is a springboard that helps you leap forward and take action towards achieving your set goals, living out your dreams and obtaining the deepest desires of your heart. Examples of positive thoughts:

"I have a designer destiny that was created especially for me."

"I can change my mind and change my destiny."

"I can live a life filled with purpose and meaning."

First, begin with some self-assessment and reflection. You can start by answering the following questions:

What is my designer destiny?

____

____

____

What is my special purpose in life?

____

____

____

What have I been assigned to do on this Earth?

____

____

____

Second, use the following techniques to cultivate positive thoughts and embed them in your mind.

- **EVALUATE** – Evaluate and assess the thoughts that come into your mind. Be certain that you focus on and pay close attention to the thoughts that are healthy in nature. Be sure to keep positive cognitions at the forefront of your mind.

- **ENGAGE** – Engage in positive self-talk that promotes a healthy and optimistic thought process. Have an internal dialogue with yourself and speak statements that will motivate, encourage and inspire you to think in a positive manner. Tell yourself that you have a designer destiny and you will fulfill it.

- **EMPLOY** – Employ and use affirmations to guide your positive thoughts. Write the affirmations on post-it notes, index cards or colorful note cards. Then strategically place them in your home, car or office so they are easily visible. Also, write them on a small piece of paper that can be kept in a planner, purse, wallet or briefcase. Repeat the affirmations until you can recite them from memory.

Identify three healthy thoughts that are related to your destiny and life purpose. Evaluate, engage and employ each of the positive thoughts.

Positive Thought #1

____

____

Positive Thought #2

____

____

Positive Thought #3

____

____

Plucking the Weeds

Your beautiful garden is vibrant and thriving, and all of a sudden the weeds begin to pop up! The weeds represent your negative thoughts that can harm and even destroy your positive thoughts. Thinking negatively can cause damage to your mentality and choke the life out of your flowers, causing your positive thoughts to wither and eventually die. Negative thoughts may cause you to be doubtful, become discouraged, lose hope and give up altogether. Unhealthy thinking can hinder you from walking in your destiny and living a life that is purposeful and filled with meaning. Therefore, it is very important to pluck the negative thoughts when they appear in your mind. Cutting these weeds prevents them from invading your garden and makes room for the flowers to grow and thrive in a healthy environment. Examples of negative thoughts are:

"I don't have a designer destiny."

"I will never fulfill my destiny."

These kinds of thoughts will certainly sabotage your destiny. Underneath the negative thinking lie irrational core beliefs which will need to be challenged and changed. Challenging your beliefs and changing your thinking helps to improve self-esteem, increase confidence, reduce anxiety and decrease fear. Ridding your mind of negative thoughts also provides a more positive outlook on life where you are filled with hope, courage and confidence. First, identify and evaluate any negative core beliefs and underlying assumptions by asking yourself the following questions:

What negative belief(s) do I hold related to my destiny?

____

____

Where did my belief(s) come from?

____

____

Why am I making this assumption?

____

____

Second, use the following techniques to challenge and change the unhealthy core beliefs that you hold.

- **DISPUTE** – Dispute and debate the irrational core beliefs. Disagree with the negative thought that pops into your mind and make an argument as to why the belief is not rational.
- **DISPROVE** – Search for evidence of whether the core belief is true or false. If there is no evidence that the belief is 100% true, prove that the negative thoughts are false, inaccurate, erroneous or wrong.
- **DISPLANT** – Remove and replace the negative thoughts with positive thoughts. Think of healthy, adaptive thoughts that can be used as alternatives to the maladaptive thoughts.

Identify three negative thoughts that are related to your destiny and life purpose. Dispute, disprove and displant each of the negative thoughts.

Negative Thought #1

____

____

Negative Thought #2

____

____

Negative Thought #3

____

____

Changing your mindset is a process, and it will not be quick and easy. It will take time to transform your thinking, and you will certainly have to work at it. Your beliefs and thoughts will not automatically change or be corrected overnight or next week. First, make the decision that you will challenge your current beliefs and change your current thinking patterns. Second, set a goal that you will replace any negative, unhealthy thoughts with thoughts that are positive and healthy. Third, create an action plan that outlines the steps you will take to accomplish this goal. Lastly, use the following advice and tips to help you with the task of transforming your mentality:

- Pray and ask God to help you with the transformation of your mind.
- Invest time, energy and effort to change your mentality.
- Practice positive thinking and self-talk on a daily basis.
- Keep a journal to record your rational beliefs and positive thoughts.
- Reward yourself when you notice positive changes in your thoughts, feelings and actions.

It is never too late to change your mentality, beginning with your underlying core beliefs and conscious thoughts. Now is the perfect time to begin the transformation of your mind so you can discover the pathway that leads to your designer destiny and will help you live your life to the fullest. You do not have to wait until tomorrow or the next day, you can begin making the mental changes today. Taking the necessary steps to challenge and change your mindset will help you begin the journey to fulfill your unique purpose in life. Empower yourself through your mind by letting positive thinking guide you along the way as you pursue your special life purpose. YOUR DIVINE DESTINY IS WAITING FOR YOU! I leave you with this one last thought and want you to BELIEVE IT, THINK IT, FEEL IT, and SPEAK IT:

CHANGE YOUR MIND TO CHANGE YOUR DESTINY!!

Recommended Reading

The Bible

The Power of Positive Thinking by Norman Vincent Peale

Managing Your Mind: The Mental Fitness Guide by Gillian Butler, Ph.D., and Tony Hope, M.D.

Notes:

ABOUT THE AUTHOR

Lee Ann Grubbs

Lee Ann Grubbs is currently studying to become a certified life coach; empowering woman to discover their self worth, help them set and obtain future goals and learn that they control their own destiny. She will also specialize in all types of relationships- both personal and marriage.

Every aspect of our lives involves relationships. Guiding people to make their relationships harmonious, peaceful, balanced and fulfilled will be the focus of Lee Ann's coaching; in both individual relationship and marriage relationships.

There is a significant contrast between coaching and counseling. Coaching is about being a mentor. It involves asking the right questions to help the client become empowered so they can create their own customized plan to help them create the success they want. This is accomplished through improved communication, focus and accountability. Coaching increases the client's abilities to accomplish more on their own. It does not give the client only one solution; it increases the client's ability to continually develop solutions continuously. Lee Ann is passionate about helping people discover their passion for life, empowering people to be the best they can be, helping people learn healthy relationship skills so that unhealthy relationships can become a part of the past. Coaching is about being a mentor.

Her accomplishments include: Who's Who of America-Multiple Sales Recognition

2001, 100% Club Sales Award (For Mutliple Years) for giving 100%, Top Associate Sales Award (Multiple Quarters), Top Producer Award & Nominated for Rookie Realtor of the Year, Nominated for Texas Realtor Leadership Program.

Her Professional Affiliations include ASI- Advertising Specialty Institute, Odessa Board of Realtors, Education Committee, Community Service Community Chairperson and Woman Council of Realtors Vice President for Retention and Recruitment.

In addition, Lee Ann is a Licensed Realtor in Texas. She has been in sales for 12 years and taught elementary school for 7 years (Physical Education, 5th Grade, 6th Grade, & ESL as well as being cheerleading sponsor. She holds a Bachelor's degree from Angelo State University.

Born and raised in Texas. She has lived throughout the state, furthering her career in sales and supporting her husband's career. In her spare time Lee Ann enjoys reading and writing. She loves redecorating homes; both hers and acquaintances and traveling, in the US and overseas. She has a passion for helping those in need.

Contact:
Lee Ann Grubbs
432-634-0693
lagrubbs1@gmail.com

TWENTY-THREE

No Matter Your Past, The Future is Yours

By Lee Ann Grubbs

"We become what we think about all day long."—Earl Nightingale

Are you ready to put the past behind you and start living a more satisfying, fulfilling life? You have the power to change your thought process, therefore allowing yourself to live your life to its fullest potential.

Forgiveness is the first step in letting go of your past and start living for today. This is about *you*, for you, it has nothing to do with the other person. You need to forgive yourself and forgive the person who wronged you. To start forgiving yourself and feeling better about who you are say the following affirmation out loud with confidence and repeat it 3 times; each time say it a little louder and with more self confidence.

I forgive myself. I let go of the past and am looking forward to today. I know with all of my heart that I am special and I deserve the best life has to offer. I love myself and am loved. I am happy and feel excited about my life. My relationships are harmonious, healthy, fulfilling, peaceful, satisfying and mutual. Throughout the day my thoughts will be positive. I know that to a large extent, I control my present and my future.

After saying the affirmation three times, do you feel better, more confident? Write the affirmation on a sticky note, put it somewhere where you will see it several times a day; maybe on your bathroom mirror. Say the affirmation over and over again until you feel it, you believe it and it becomes a part of you. Every time you look at the affirmation, read it or say it out loud until you have it memorized so you can repeat it to yourself when you are in a stressful situation and need to have a calming presence about you.

When you learn to forgive yourself, give yourself permission to no longer feel guilty and learn to love yourself, it will be like a breath of fresh air. This takes time, and you will have to do this over and over again, but it is achievable.

Our next step is to work through forgiving the person towards whom you have a grudge. You might be asking yourself, "Why should I forgive *that* person?" The answer is simple… as long as you hold on to any grudges or resentment towards that person, he/she has a power over you. When you resent someone and they have a power over you, do you realize it does not affect them. Yet it affects many aspects of your life. It affects your life in a negative way. Until you have truly forgiven that person, you not only give them the power to influence how you feel, think and act, but also quite possibly it can have a powerful effect on your physical health – stress eating, obesity, diabetes, cancer, fibromyalgia, or other diseases that may be linked to stress.

Until you let go of the past and forgive, the situation will have a strong hold on you; it will negatively affect most of your relationships – work, your home life, friends, but most importantly your belief about yourself. When you have decided it is in your best interest to *truly* forgive someone, it can be very liberating.

Before you begin the exercises it is imperative to understand what true forgiveness is and what it is not. True forgiveness is strictly for you and only you. It literally has *nothing* to do with the other person. You are the *only one* who is taking action; you cannot expect anything from the other person. In all reality, it has to be unconditional. It is essential that you understand this. The person you are choosing to forgive has *nothing* to do with your choice to forgive them.

You might still be thinking, "Why should I forgive him/her? They do not deserve it!" This could be very true. You may feel that they owe you an apology, an explanation…something; *anything*. If they would give you this, you would be able to forgive them. That again could be true. But, remember you are doing this for you, not for them, so you cannot *require* anything of them. This step can be very difficult to do because you might feel like you are letting them off the hook, or that you are telling them that their actions were OK. But in reality, what you are saying is I choose to forgive you, although what you did to me was not OK. It was wrong, but I choose to free you from any revenge I feel I owe you. Again, accomplishing this step can be both difficult and very liberating. Throughout your life you will often have to revisit this. It does not happen overnight.

As before, write this down and repeat it to yourself out loud 3 times, each time a little louder and with a little more confident.

I choose to forgive _____(name of the person) and break free of the bonds that hold me back. _____(name of the person) no longer has control of my life. I know in my heart that the issues that caused_____(name of the person) to offend me are due to their issues and problems. This is not about me; it is not personal.

Repeat it anytime you feel resentment towards someone and you know it is time to let go of these negative feelings.

You will know you have fully forgiven that person when you can think about that person, hear their name or see them and have no negative thoughts or reactions towards them. No anger, no resentment. This is a wonderful feeling. Again, it is not always an easy task, but once accomplished and you realize you have forgiven someone who has wronged you, it may feel like having a ton of bricks removed from your shoulders or it might feel like you are as light as a feather.

It is up to you to choose to forgive, but once you do it is exhilarating to be able to say I have reclaimed responsibility and power in my life.

Forgiving and forgetting are two different things. You have heard people say forgive and forget, but in some cases it is ok to not forget. You would not want another incident like this to affect you again. Learn to forgive, not necessarily forget so you can keep this person from having the opportunity to do this or something similar to you again. But go on with your life. The goal here is to reach a point where there is not the emotional baggage that ruled your life in the past. Your goal is to be able to think about that person and not feel any negative emotion.

Part of getting perfect balance in your life is learning to forgive yourself and others and letting go of past hurts.

This is an exercise to discover whether we have forgiven and/ or discover if we need to work more on inner thoughts. Take a few minutes and think of a situation from your past that has a hold on you. It may be something that happened five minutes ago, last year or in your childhood. It could be something as simple as a conversation you had with someone, a 'friend' or family member saying something hurtful, a specific event; anything where the outcome was not what you hoped it would be. A situation that left you feeling insecure, unsatisfied, empty, baffled, not good enough, or like the example above thinking to yourself, why did I say that? Write this down:

How did the situation make you feel:

Ask yourself, "Was this really about me or was it about the other person's issues?"

More than likely, you will find that it really is the other person's issue, not yours. If it was truly about the other person, choose to forgive them and let it go. On the other hand, if it was due to your internal issues, you have some work to do. You need to reprogram your thought process about your worthiness. We will discover how to do this next!

Learning to Retrain What You Say to Yourself to Live Your Best Life Possible

What you think and feel to a large degree determines your future. When you finally are able to let go of the victim stories that haunt you as a person you will be able to reclaim your life and take back your power. You will start attracting more positive people into your life, your feelings will not be hurt so easily, you will have much less stress and be a much happier person.

Think about the following situation: Two different people are going to receive the exact same evaluation at work. They are each praised for their contribution and given the same three suggestions for areas of improvement. The verbiage, tone and atmosphere are identical in each meeting. The only difference in the two scenarios is the attitude and belief system of the two people being evaluated.

Tina is excited about her upcoming evaluation. Waking up full of energy, looking forward to the upcoming day she goes to work and at the appointed time goes to the evaluation. The evaluation goes as well as could be expected, and she leaves the meeting excited! Her boss has complimented her on her various accomplishments throughout the year as well as giving her three areas to concentrate on next year. Overflowing with excitement, she immediately goes to her office to begin working on next year's goals and figuring out how to incorporate the suggested areas for improvement into her yearly goals and plan.

Mary, on the other hand, wakes up with a headache, she had trouble sleeping last night and is anxious about today's evaluation. Throughout the morning she thinks about the evaluation and hopes it goes well, but in the back of her mind she's worried about what her boss is going to say. During the evaluation she feels jubilant when her boss compliments her on her accomplishments, but this feeling is short lived. As they discuss the areas that she can improve on her mood deflates. When she leaves the meeting she is feels down and wonders how she is going to meet the demands her boss has put on her. As she enters her office she starts thinking maybe it's time to find another job and a boss who would appreciate all of her hard work.

Let's explore why two people can have the exact same experience but come away feeling completely different.

Tina was raised in a loving, nurturing and caring family. There were always lots of hugs, lots of laughter and a tremendous amount of encouragement. When she would dance and be goofy around her parents they would always laugh, clap and carry on about how wonderful she was. They showered her with praise and love. When she would make a mistake or did something 'bad' she was not scolded harshly or told she was dumb. Instead, she was told to think about what she was saying or doing and was asked if that was the proper way to behave. Her mother usually would not just tell her why it was wrong, she would talk to her in a way that made her understand and Tina would be able to tell her mother in her own words why it was wrong. Consequently, she was constantly saying to herself through her inner thoughts, I am wonderful, I am confident, I can do anything.

Mary, on the other hand, was raised in a much different environment. Her parents worked long hours and basically did not have energy left at the end of the day for Mary and her siblings. As many children do when they get excited about something, she would run inside to tell her mom or dad something wonderful that happened in her day. She was often told not now, tell me later and then they would ask her something like, "Did you clean your room?" or "Have you taken the trash out?" She was a very vibrant and bright child but as the years went on, she withdrew into a shell. The message she got from home was I am not good enough, I am not worthy. Nothing I do will ever be good enough. She goes throughout her life with these messages playing continuously in her mind. She starts to believe them, they become her reality and it effects every aspect of her life.

Our past situations affect what we think and how we feel. It would be nice if every child in the world could be raised in a home like Tina's, but unfortunately that is not the case. The good news is Mary can retrain her brain to think like Tina's. Even better still, so can you. It is not easy, but with determination and perseverance you can rerecord the inner thoughts that play over and over again inside your head.

Once you realize the chaos negative energy creates in your life, you let go of the victim stories and reclaim your life. You take your power back! It is exhilarating!

Exercise: Set aside this book for 10 to 15 minutes. Go about doing chores or your daily routine. As you are performing these tasks, pay close attention to what you are saying to yourself. Were your thoughts positive or negative?

____

____

Say the following affirmation:

I am a wonderful person. I deserve the best in life and will attract positive things in all aspects of my life. I am lovable and I am the best person I can be. I can do anything I set my mind to.

Repeat this statement three times. How do you feel after saying that to yourself? Do you feel more peaceful? Now, put aside the book again for 10 to 15 minutes and resume your chores or everyday routine. Again, pay close attention to what you are saying to yourself about yourself.

This time were your inner thoughts more positive?

Learning to take negative inner thoughts out of our life is not an easy task to accomplish and it does not happen overnight. Every time you catch yourself being negative STOP, take a deep breath and say something positive about yourself! There will be days you will have to stop and regroup five times in one hour while other days will be a breeze and you may only have to say the affirmation one time in the morning. The longer you do this the easier it becomes and the easier it is to change your thoughts and feelings about yourself. When you start to accomplish this you will be amazed at the powerful impact it has on your life.

If Mary had been paying attention to her inner thoughts and changed her negative thoughts to positive thoughts throughout the morning, her feelings toward herself, her evaluation and her life would have been completely different.

We have talked a lot about healing your mind. Let's take a minute to discuss your body and wellness. Did you know that heart disease is the #1 killer in woman? Techniques like the one above have been proven to reduce your cortisol levels. A lot of stress day in and day out adds up over time and increases your chance of developing serious health problems.

You can do this! You have the power to *change* your life! Make up your mind to and never say or accept the words I CAN'T. If you say you can't, you are right, you won't be able to do what you have set out to do. If you say and believe I CAN, you are also right, you can and you will. You just have to believe in yourself and you can accomplish anything you set your mind to.

Exercise: Take a 5 minute break away from reality and complete the following relaxation exercise. I suggest you do this several times throughout your day. It will greatly help reduce your stress level. Sit down; sit up straight. Close your eyes. Take 7 very deep breaths, breathing in through your nose and letting the air out through your mouth. Visualize you are walking down a serene path next to a river. Hear the water from the bubbling creek. Each step you take relaxes you more and more.

Things to do to help create positive thoughts and bring you more peace.

- If you are a believer, PRAY.
- A friend attributes this activity alone to helping her change her inner thoughts and changing her entire life. She put a CD player in her bathroom. Every morning she listens to a motivational speaker as she is getting ready for her day. Some examples of amazing motivational speakers are Joel Osteen (minister), Clay Nelson, Stephen Covey, Dale Carnegie.
- Listen to books on CD while driving or read books by motivational speakers.
- Anytime you feel stressed, say positive affirmations to yourself. Find the ones that motivate you the most, write these down, put them in a prominent place and repeat them to yourself often.

- Listen to relaxing, calming music.
- Turn off the TV and listen to music that picks you up and makes you feel good.
- Make a commitment to spend 15 to 30 minutes a day to just take care of you. Read a motivational or self-help book on a topic you feel you need to work on.

ABOUT THE AUTHOR

Dr. Veronica Eddy

Dr. Veronica Eddy, President of Dove Consulting and Counseling Group, LLC, is as RN, who earned a BA in Psychology from St Leo University in St Leo, Florida. She earned a Masters in Religious Arts, was ordained into ministry, and continued on to earn her PhD and NCCA licensure as a clinical pastoral counselor from Jacksonville Theological Seminary.

Her nursing career has spanned more than forty-six years with half of that spent working in the Oncology field where she not only administered chemotherapy and counseled patients and their families through very difficult times, but also helped families through the death of their loved ones.

Dr. Eddy has also worked as an administrative assistant in a successful nursing company providing IV services to the nursing home communities around the state of Florida, as well as in MD., VA., Washington D.C., and other regions of the Northeast. Her ability to understand and relate to women in this highly stressful environment keeps her continually in the forefront of providing the necessary tools to work smarter, not harder. About two years ago, she has relocated to Pennsylvania, is working as an Intake Coordinator in a growing home health agency and continues to attend to the needs of the nurses under her care.

Professionally, she is a member of the National Association of Professional Nurses (NAPN), a Certified Trainer with Professional Woman Network specializing in the area of Women's Issues, is a member of The American Association of Christian Counselors (AACC), and The National Christian Counselors Association (NCCA).

Dr. Eddy has had the privilege of being the women's ministry leader in her church in Florida where she applied her expertise in the many areas of the needs of women. She has also designed and implemented a grief recovery program to minister to the countless people needing support after experiencing loss, as well as help to train others to help those in the depths of their grief. After her relocation, she continues to be involved in her church singing on the praise team and ministering to wounded and grieving women. As a licensed clinical pastoral counselor, her understanding of one's emotional needs propel her forward to help minister to and help meet the needs of the physically and spiritually battered women.

Contact:
123 Carriage Dr.
North Huntingdon, Pa. 15642
727-247-7944 or 724-989-9311
Email: dccgroup07@aol.com

TWENTY-FOUR

Rebuilding After Tragedy

By Dr. Veronica Eddy

"Of all the liars in the world, sometimes the worst are your own fears."
—Rudyard Kipling

Tragedy can take many forms and when it strikes, fear usually isn't far behind. Tragedy is usually associated with the physical parameters of our lives, but in reality, it encompasses so much more. Tragedy denotes loss and the losses primarily thought of are our homes and possessions after some act of nature such as a flood, hurricane or earthquake. But the losses can also be a result of divorce, loss of one's physical health, a job loss or the tragic loss of a spouse or child. Because of these losses, many more tangible items are lost as well, and the energy and emotional strength required to replace them is enormous.

What are some of the tangible losses you have experienced?

1. ____

2. ____

3. ____

What have you discovered about the amount of energy/emotional strength required to rebuild?

1. ____

2. ____

3. ____

As a result of these tangible losses, many intangible losses occur, as well. They can't be seen or touched as can the physical, but are every bit as real and potentially disabling. Loss of inner peace, loss of hope and joy, loss of self-esteem, lost confidence and lack of energy are some of the emotions – those intangibles – that are experienced and need attended to in order to move forward to begin the rebuilding process. In this process the old and bad are taken away and the new and better and stronger replace it. However, we cannot go down to the nearest realtor, contractor or department store to replace and rebuild our emotions, our energy, or our confidence. We cannot sit and look in the mirror and convince ourselves that all is OK with us and our world. This despair and these emotions can be more destructive than any physical loss we may experience. And through it all, we must continue to put one foot in front of the other, continue to move forward, go to our jobs and perform, come home again to care for our families and do all the other things necessary to make it through the day. You may be thinking to yourself that your loss(es) isn't much, but it is important to realize that many of these intangible losses can arise and cling to just one tangible loss. One loss can turn a life upside down, creating immense turmoil and the spiral deepens to a place that seems impossible to get out of. It may even become a vicious cycle of spiraling down, rebounding for a period of time, but then spiraling down again. The rebound place is never as high as it was previously because the downward spiral is even deeper. The result of these losses can create emotions of despair that are very devastating and long term, not to mention potentially self-destructive.

When we lose our *inner peace,* many emotions fight for our attention. Some of them that come to mind are:

- The inability to concentrate – lost focus
- Increased sensitivity to words spoken – faulty interpretation/perception
- Second guessing our decisions or decision making ability
- Fear
- Inner turmoil
- Feelings of inadequacy
- Guilt
- Anxiety
- Depression

- Resentment
- Unforgiveness

When we lose our *hope and joy*, we are bombarded with yet another array of emotions. Some of these may include:

- Despair
- Depression – hovering like a horrid rain cloud, never moving or dissipating
- Wanting to give up and forget about ever trying again
- Denial
- Arrogance – a defense mechanism to keep people away
- Lost energy
- Lost vision for the future
- Suicidal intent

Our loss of *self-esteem* becomes a major player on this field of intangibles. One reason may be because we have never recognized that it was low or nonexistent to begin with and now this tragedy has shattered our glass bubble pretense of our view of ourselves. Self-esteem is a feeling of value, worth and pride in oneself; a self-assurance, self-regard, self-respect and self-love, if you will. It encompasses so much of who we are, how we see ourselves, as well as how we present ourselves. This concept of self-love is spoken of by Jesus Christ in the Gospel of

Mark (12:31), to "love our neighbor as ourselves." My understanding of this is that without self-love, loving others can be very difficult.

In light of this, what range of destructive emotions may be exhibited? They may include:

- Shyness
- Excessive people pleasing
- Inability to speak up or stand up for oneself
- Excessive dependence on others
- Oversensitivity to criticism
- Need to control
- Addictions – alcohol, drugs, food, shopping, sex
- Victim mentality
- Guilt
- Self-blame
- Self-mutilation – may include anorexia, cutting, pulling out hair to name a few
- Co-dependency – depending on others for self-worth
- Fear
- Shame

Of course, this list is not all inclusive but it is a starting place to allow you to begin your journey to rebuild after your tragedy; a tragedy that doesn't necessarily have to be a recent one but could lay buried under years of scars and life just needing to be lived. The rebuilding process begins with taking inventory to discover the areas needing repair, the necessary costs involved and the time needed to be invested. The entire cost must be determined, whether it be a physical rebuilding or an emotional one. Burying our pain and emotions can be its own form of self-preservation. But eventually it must be faced, dealt with and the emotional cost considered. Will you be willing to pay the price to be whole and emotionally healthy?

Go back and review these lists and mark the ones that you recognize as having experienced and still may carry some weight in how you get through every day. Be prepared to experience some discomfort in this process; proceed slowly, if necessary, and please be kind and gentle to yourself. Please realize that this is the first step in healing and rebuilding – identifying those emotions/attitudes that have enveloped you in a "protective (really a destructive) shell" all these years. Don't be surprised how raw some of those emotions can be, emotions that you felt were long forgotten. Also, be willing to be brutally honest with this evaluation process. Remember, pain is healthy since it is a sign that something is not right. It must be looked at as a positive sign to be investigated, not something to push away and ignore because of its discomfort.

As you look over these lists, what are still the strongest emotions and how have they impacted your life to date? Briefly identify these emotions and describe how you felt/feel. (A journal may be helpful as you begin this journey because these few lines here won't even begin to be enough.)

____

____

____

You may want to ask yourself:

1. When I identified______________________________, I experienced______________________________ again/or for the first time.

2. What incident(s) or person(s) came to mind as I reviewed and identified this/these emotion(s)?

   ____

3. Was/were it/they positive or negative emotion(s)/experience(s) and how did it/they affect my future choice(s)?

   ____

4. Were my choices my own or did I allow others to take over?

   ____

   If I did, am I still being controlled/influenced by others?

   ____

5. Have I ever taken responsibility for what happened, if the responsibility was mine?

____

6. Did I view this past issue in my life as my patterned destiny and allow it to rule everything else?

____

7. Did I feel I deserved to have happen to me what happened and/or to be treated the way I was?

____

This is *very* important to explore because it is a victim mentality and successful rebuilding cannot be accomplished while remaining a victim. We must move from victim to victor.

There are many, many more questions that can be asked and that will be up to you to search out as you begin this process of restoration and rebuilding.

In my time of rebuilding, one of the most important questions asked of me by my counselor was, "Tell me who you are?" WOW! That really opened up a hornet's nest of issues. Why? Because I had no answer. I never thought of who I really was, of what was important to me or if I really was anyone at all. It wasn't until my intense loss/tragedy at middle age that I began my journey of discovering who I was and what I was. There was intense pain when I discovered I had no personal identity except what was attached to my profession. All I knew was that I was a nurse, but nothing else. I had no individual identity. I had no direction for this nonperson I believed I was. I saw and thought very little, if anything, of myself except to wake up, get dressed, and go to work, come home, go to bed and start all over again the next day just putting one foot in front of the other with no identity or destiny. Why? Because my identity was always someone else's – their life, their dreams, their future. Also, I had made choices that were not the best and they added to the process of lost self-respect and lost self-esteem.

However, through the loss, despair and seeming tragedy, with God's love and direction and many wonderful friends I became the phoenix rising out of the ashes of despair to become who God created me to be – His unique creation with individual gifts, talents and skills. A verse of scripture was given to me and became very important to me at this time. It is found in Jeremiah 29:11. "I know the plans I have for you, declares the Lord, plans to prosper you and not to harm you, plans to give you a hope and a future." (NIV)

Because we are thrust into an arena of many unknowns, being frightened seems to overpower our physical senses, our self-esteem, our imaginations and even our common sense. But we cannot allow our fears to overrule what we know what we must do, can do and aspire to do. There is no barrier so great that we cannot overcome. We must learn to dwell on solutions rather than the problems and learn to be optimists rather than pessimists. The journey to restoration and rebuilding is not easy, nor is it accomplished overnight. We self-sabotage very easily and sometimes the energy needed to pull ourselves up is almost nonexistent. But when we believe – and that is what we must do – believe that we have worth and value, then we can make that journey with strength and courage. Convincing ourselves that we are worthy is a daily endeavor after years, or even a lifetime, of being told or shown how little we are valued. With God all things are possible. As I observe the magnificent movement of dance, listen to the exquisite sounds of song and taste the delicate flavors of a well prepared meal, I am constantly amazed at the great things we can achieve as we press forward in our desires and dreams.

You must learn and begin to take personal responsibility for your present and future destiny. Recognizing what is important and standing by those convictions will empower you to rise above defeat and begin or continue this journey to rebuilding your life. Care must be taken not to allow others to undermine your goals and new found confidence. Those used to controlling you and your past needy life will not like losing that control. You have control over your own life and the power to chart the course you choose to travel. On that journey, do not ever allow anyone to attempt to squash your dreams. Never allow negative people to speak over you and begin to fill you with doubt and despair. Surround yourself with friends and people who believe in you and your rebuilding process, people who are encouragers and will allow you to become who you were created to be.

We are all fearfully and wonderfully made and have been given gifts and talents to be discovered and cultivated. When you think you have nothing to offer, just look inside. We are all given a measure of faith (Romans 12:33). That isn't there just to believe God for physical healing or the meeting of a financial need, but with that measure of faith we can step into our dream, and in spite of the roadblocks, which will inevitably present themselves, keep pressing on to see its birth and development.

Notes:

ABOUT THE AUTHOR

Thelma D. Abney

Thelma Abney co-owns 'Swagg'n 2000 LPC (Doing Something I Believe I Can!) She and her business partner conduct workshops throughout the state of New Jersey, reaching out to the Youth with the most rewarding topic of Self-Esteem. Ms. Abney has been certified by The Professional Woman Network as a Professional Youth Coach.

Ms. Abney's knowledge of business and professionalism is supported by working with non-profit and charity -based organizations. She has 5 ½ years experience working in Juvenile Corrections as well as 5 years of experience working in the Adult Correction Facility. She has been The President of the Junior Usher Board for over 5 years at the church she attends.

Among her many accomplishments, Thelma Abney has co-authored a book, "The Power of Change: Reinventing yourself At Any Age". She holds a Certificate in computers from Devry Technology, and Certificates in Gang Recognition in the United States.

Book

- The Power of Change. Reinventing Yourself At Any Age

Certifications

- Certified Professional Youth Coach
- State of NJ Commission Juveniles Justice
- State of NJ Criminal Justice Police Commission

Professional Organizations

- The Professional Woman Network
- NJDA JJC

Contact:
Website: www.Swagg'n2000.org
Email: Swagg'n2000@aol.com

TWENTY-FIVE

From Debt to Wealth: New Money Habits

By Thelma D. Abney

Start Saving

Saving money is a way of life. But most people would agree that saving money is something that is easier said than done. The biggest challenge about saving is not being in the **habit!** It all starts by paying yourself *first* by directly depositing money from your paycheck into your saving account. If you don't have a savings account then inquire about opening an account today! Taking care of yourself is not secondary to everyone else. You deserve to have financial security that is all yours and that you know you can always rely upon in a personal emergency. The smartest way to build your savings account is to set up a system where you authorize the bank to automatically transfer money each month from your checking to your saving account. You won't have to remember to put money in your savings account, and you won't be able to make any excuses when you feel like spending rather than saving. By setting up an automatic electronic monthly transfer, you are forcing yourself to save. You can choose the auto-deposit option when you sign up for a saving account. It takes sacrifice to gain financial security by building a large saving account.

We all have change in coins laying around the house, in a dresser drawer or in the car. Start filling a jar with your left-over change. When you return home from shopping, drop that spare change from your pocket into your money jar. When your jar get full you will be surprise about the money that you saved! Deposit this change into you saving account and just watch it grow even more. Keep filling that jar to the brim!

Most people have a checking account before they have a savings account. But if you don't have a checking account its important to open one as soon as possible. Your checking account should be for one purpose only and that should be for bill paying. It is not where you keep money you are saving to open your own business or a down payment on a house. However, oftentimes women do not look at their checking account statement and just hope they have enough money in the bank to cover the bills. Take responsibly in balancing your checkbook every month!

A Good Checking Account has:

1. No monthly fee for having the account
2. A low required balance to qualify for free checking

3. Free checks and check writing
4. Online access to your account statements and free online bill pay
5. Insurance coverage of your deposits

Let's Talk Credit Cards! Potential for Trouble

Let's start with your debt. Many people get into a lot of debt with credit cards. The more credit cards you have the more money you will spend, *especially if you are a compulsive shopper.* Most "shopaholics" are women who often go on shopping sprees to make themselves feel good, and might be depressed or upset with their partners. This is their immediate 'feel good' behavior when times are tough. But once the credit cards pay for the shopping, thirty days later their debits increase with the arrival of their credit card bill! **A word of advice: Do not shop with your credit card! Leave your credit card at home. In fact, if you are married, ask your partner to hold your credit card and discuss purchases before you use the card again! Shop with CASH! Pay for only that which you can afford.** If you have an online account with a department store, remove your credit information because it's an easy way to spend money online – just click and buy (and rack up more debt!). Credit cards are made to keep you in debt if you don't use them carefully and wisely. Most people carry monthly balances. In the long run with the interest rate you end up paying double or triple for the same item rather than paying off the bill monthly. **The banks make A LOT of money by you paying only the minimum. They are depending upon you NOT to pay off your balance. Remember, your credit card is a 'debtor's card' and makes banks rich and you**

POOR. (Were those shoes or purse that serious sisters that you went into increased debt by impulsive spending? Save for these items and then spend **cash**! By the way, men tend to use credit cards to 'big ticket' item such as electronics, televisions, etc. They tend not to be impulse buyers in comparison to women.

A lot of people get their first credit card in their late teens or early twenties (especially if you are in college) and the credit card company offerings arrive fast and furiously! The deals are too good to be true and you might find yourself $15,000 in debt before you're twenty-five!

Decline those offers, ladies! In fact, now is the time to reduce ALL your credit cards to one ONLY! (Yes, it's time to get rid of all those department store credit cards, as well.) Cut them up and carry no more than one credit card for **emergency use only** and start paying off your balance every month. Credit cards give you maximum control over spending urges. Your focus should be on *your needs* rather than *your wants.* **If you can't control your spending, then don't own a credit card**!

Clothes Shopping

If you are a big spender on clothing, especially the designers, then you are probably familiar with the name brand manufactures such as Prado, Gucci, Ralph Lauren, Calvin Klein, Betsy Johnson, Armani, Nike, Liz Claiborne, etc., that operate their own independent stores offering discounts up to 50% to the public who are looking for sales and bargains. A tip: set a budget and stay within that budget! Buy clothes that can be accessorized for different looks, thus spreading your wardrobe dollars even farther. The importance of that simple black dress that can be worn to the office, dinner, clubs, shows, church or a funeral, can be accessorized with different scarves, pins, and necklaces to achieve a new look. **Remember–clothes shopping should be a form of entertainment! Teens learn this habit at a young age by watching their mothers and peers shopping for items they really don't NEED.** Many women (and teens) fall into the trip of feeling the need to HAVE the newest and the hottest trends that come out, no matter what! This includes clothes, shoes, boots, sneakers, laptops, computers, phones, purses, hairstyles, make-up etc. These same women and teens are increasing their debit constantly by spending what they don't have, just to keep up appearances! Television shows like BET, MTV, VH1 Atlanta Housewives, Basketball Housewives and many other reality shows can actually increase spending by women as they want to look like these celebrities with their clothing, jewelry, tattoos, and did I forget plastic surgery, the hottest new trend that sweeping the nation? Cosmetic surgery is a very high ticket item for all ages and yes, most women place this surgical bill on their plastic credit card! More debt! Remember, one big way to save money is to watch less television or turn off the television so there will be less exposure to guilt-inducing ads.

Grocery Shopping

Make a grocery list before you go to the store that is for a two-week meal plan. This may sound obvious to some of you, but many shoppers go up and down the grocery aisles simply loading their carts with items that catch their eye, regardless if the item is on sale or not, buying impulse items, and not comparing prices. Not only should you have a list, but you should **never shop while you're hungry!** Truly, you could end up buying twice as much what you have on your shopping list. (**Hunger = Impulse Buying**) Avoid 'touring' the aisles that aren't on your list. If you know your grocery store layout, make notes on your list as to the aisle numbers and stick to them! How about saving money by learning a new hobby such a gardening and learning to grown your own herbs and vegetables. (You'll be amazed at the taste compared to store-bought veggies which may be shipped from out-of-state or in some cases such as fruit, shipped from another country!) Do your best to support locally grown produce and visit your Farmer's Market! The produce is fresh frozen at peak ripeness, so it will taste better than crops shipped from miles away and it will cost much less. Start shopping sales (Whole Foods often sells two-for-one fresh soups on Wednesdays; in some stores there is a special 'senior citizen' day which offers substantial discounts on groceries). Buy the Sunday newspaper. It's a great way to save money as it offers food brand coupons. (Clip all the coupons on products you use the most and the new products you would like to try. Holding off on using coupons until the item goes on sale is an easy way to double or triple your savings. Be on the lookout for "double coupon" days.) One of the best kitchen investments is a deep freezer for those 'marked down' items. (Make room in your pantry, too for those sale items!) Avoid non-grocery items that can be bought elsewhere such as Wal-Mart, Target or Walgreens.

Five Rules for Grocery Shopping:

1. Go shopping alone.
2. Have a budget, make your list and stick to it.
3. Don't shop hungry.

4. Buy the Sunday newspaper.

5. Use coupons.

The more you save the more you can get out of debt!

Your Car

Gasoline is expensive, so remember to lighten the load of your car when possible. You can reduce the mass of your car by emptying out the trunk of you car. By removing heavy items that you don't need, you will have room for a spare tire, car jack, change of clothes, blanket and some tools in case of emergency. You can help your car's gasoline efficiency by maintaining service such as replacing your air filters and not using the air conditioner unless absolutely necessary. (The compressor of the air conditioner strains the motor of the car which will reduce your fuel economy.) When possible, avoid stop-and-go traffic which consumes loads of fuel. Keep your tires properly inflated as this will not only keep you safe and but save on gas mileage. (Oh, yes! Don't forget to buy your tires from Costco, Sam's Club BJ's or other wholesale clubs as they may cost a lot less than at a dealer or chain tire store!

It's In YOUR Hands!

You have the ultimate control as to whether you will remain in debt or free yourself of this financial ball and chain! Make a commitment to use a credit card less, avoid impulse shopping, and compare prices when purchasing clothing, food, automobiles, or any item which costs you money. You can live debt-free! Start today!

ABOUT THE AUTHOR

SHARON MCWILLIAMS

Having *"accidentally"* stumbled upon a miraculous second journey during her baby boomer life, Sharon McWilliams traveled into her very own Grand Wise Woman adventures, with the grand desire to use the power of an elder wise woman to make a difference in the lives of others, to selfishly focus on creating a peaceful healthy planet for her children and her grandchildren.

She took the journey of heart and soul, exploring deeply, expanding her courage muscles to continuously take just one more step. Each step of that journey pulled her deeper within, finding her own wise woman compassionate soul with natural healing and intuitive and creative abilities ready to reawaken. Sharon learned how to combine these God-given abilities with her Grand Wise Woman years of experience, honing them into the gentle wisdom place as a wise woman elder to use and share in her later years as a master Wise Woman!

Sharon is a speaker/performer, author, singer/songwriter, educator, certified retreat, life & wellness coach and Reiki Master-Teacher. A co-creator with wise women, Sharon shares her discoveries with you in her multifaceted experiential retreats and programs.

Sharon takes you on the journey of yourself with your life stories into safe retreat surroundings using compassionate playfulness. She shows you how to rediscover your natural intuition and your natural healing abilities, something all wise women have! Sharon has you rebuild and refill your wise woman toolkit, the one you forgot you had. Believe it or not, you were not put here on this planet without those wise woman tools!

"Come…retreat with me!" she says. "You can do this!"

Books:

The Power of a Woman
The Power of Change at Any Age
Celebration of Life Inspiration for Women
Daddy, I Remember Hope and Healing for Familes of Alzheimer's
Freeing Godiva A Woman's Journey of Self-Empowerment!
CSI Courageous Stories of Inspiration

Expertise:

Life, Retreat and Wellness Coaching for Women
Women and Empowerment
Personal Exploration for Women
Retreats for Wise Women
Essence Journaling
Women and their Stories
Sound Healing with Solfeggio Tuning Forks
Stress Reduction for Women

Seminars and Topics offered (also in retreat style):

Grace in Action®
The Gift of Your Stories
Your Stories are Your Music on the Journey of your Life

Wise Woman Essence Journaling

The Labyrinth Within
Retreating: the hows and whys and whens

Journaling: The Power of Presence in Writing
Visualization: The True Self Discovery Process Intuition and the Wise Woman

Contact:
The Gift
PO Box 941
Pewee Valley, KY 40056
Telephone: 502.541.3106
Email: info@thegiftlifecoach.net
Fax: 502.742.1977
Website: www.thegiftlifecoach.net
www.thegiftlifecoach.com
Blog: http://wisewomanessence.com

TWENTY-SIX

Grace in Action®

By Sharon McWilliams MEd, CLC

This is what you might call a simple treatise on the power of change for wise woman who are fifty and over. You have been gifted with a magnificent change in your body and your brain that opens doors for a new journey, a second journey of change for your true self, your spirit self, your sweet soul, so that you can be a beautiful service in this world as a wise woman elder. Menopause has long been given a bad rap, treated as an illness, medicated and made a dreaded moment for all those approaching that time. It is not so. Let me repeat that. It is not so.

Allow me to help you remember who you are and why you are here now at this time. You now carry within you a beautiful energy of creation, a wisdom that will bring you courage and cause you to take risks that you may have never done before. You are able to hold prayer energy, enough to collectively change the thinking of the world. One pure love thought overrides ninety thousand negative thoughts. And grandmothers around the world have the gifted ability to do just that, hold the sacred space for peace and the peaceful healing of our planet.

Allow me to introduce yourself to you. It is an honor to present *Grace in Action*®, a grand in action, a *grand* mother in action. Now let's move forward with some information and tools for you to step into the precious power of who you are now.

Did You Know?

- According to the U. S. Census Bureau, one out of five adults is a woman over fifty.
- Studies have shown that writing down your feelings is associated with healing of all kinds.
- A simple smile ups your endorphins.
- You should drink half your body weight in ounces of water.
- Proper breathing wards off illness and aging.
- Brain chemistry changes in midlife (similar to adolescence) with risk taking, speaking your truth and creative ventures.
- Seen in a new light, perimenopause lends itself to labor pains whereas menopause, not a disease or illness, is a powerful birthing to a masterful second journey. You have to choose the path.

Consider This:

On October 19, 2009 the Dali Lama made this statement, *"It will be the western woman who saves the world!"* An age-old Native American prophecy says, *"When the wisdom of the grandmothers is heard, the world will heal."* Alice Walker, wise woman elder and contemporary author of *The Color Purple*, entitles her latest book after the Hopi Elders' prophecy, *"We are the ones we've been waiting for!"*

This powerful yet gentle journal activity, *Grace in Action* is for you, the wise women who is at least fifty years old, having experienced menopause. You have a special purpose in life now. You remember what your gifts are; and you mold them into a purpose that will help bring a peaceful change to our planet for our children and their children's children—seven generations.

Know This:

This second journey that you are embarking on is not about the doing, for you have already done more than enough. This second journey is not about a start-up entrepreneurial business where you have to do everything yourself, yet that may create itself. This second journey is not a hobby, although your hobby may blossom.

This second journey is about your lovely spirit, your soul, the essence of who you are really. This second journey will be guided by *her*. You haven't seen *her* in a while. She has a beautiful name, that you may discover later. She is *Grace in Action*. She is you. You have only forgotten; but you will remember *her* as you retreat with me.

You also have a toolkit you have forgotten about. Heaven didn't put you here without one. This journal moment out of time will help you rebuild that kit. Are you ready for this? I know you are. That's why you're reading this chapter now. This timing is called synchronicity – guidance from above and within. Come…retreat with me on this beautiful journey of love.

So Picture This:

What if around your fiftieth year, as you experience menopause your whole life seems to turn upside down? Nothing will ever be the same. Maybe you become a caregiver for your dad who has Alzheimer's, or maybe your mother lost her will to live. You have become an empty nester. Your spouse has had a grueling quadruple by-pass and you lose more than one good friend to breast cancer. Maybe you yourself develop a critical illness or encounter a debilitating fall. You divorce, or even worse, you lose a precious child.

Does any of this ring a bell for you? Does any of this sound familiar? Does any of this bring up moments you have chosen to forget, bury, and pretend it was someone else, not you? Does any of this bring up your stories, incidents that created sadness, fear, anger, even depression? How many rugs have been pulled out from under your feet? Did you act up, act out, or swallow it? What if I give you permission to become very angry as a baby boomer woman, because this was not the plan, not the unspoken promise to a young woman of the seventies just graduating from college with such a great secure future?!!

Your New Story

What if there was another way to constructively use your anger, sadness, even depression to make a new story? What if you are determined to release what no longer works for you? What if you decide to change your course of action as an older woman? What if you decide not to lay down and forget your dreams? What if you decide to gather your courage muscle to become a powerhouse of a wise woman, *Grace in Action*? You can do this as you retreat with me. Remember this?

"Entreat me not to leave thee, for whither thou goest, I will go; whither thou lodgest, I will lodge. Thy people shall be my people; and thy God, my God." as spoken by Naomi to Ruth of the Old Testament.

Retreat – What Is It?

What do I mean by retreat? Does this have to do with church? Does it have to do with a camp? Does it have to do with a group of women? Is it like sleepovers, brownie camps, training bras? Maybe, if you want it to be.

However, I expand the definition of retreat to mean a moment out of time in a place of quiet within and without where nothing necessarily happens. Yet, peace slides in, joy comes to the forefront, and love for yourself returns a thousand-fold. (Remember how the Bible says you must love your neighbor as you love yourself – reread that last part.)

Anne Morrow Lindebergh, in her *Gift from the Sea*, mentions taking three weeks away from everything and retreating to the beach with her journal (that journal created her book). Well, it's difficult to take three weeks to retreat like she did. But, like ten minute power naps, even a ten minute retreat for yourself performs little miracles.

A retreat is where you become your very own oxygen mask, where you take charge of your life again. A retreat is a simple place of repose where you reconnect with who you are, why you are here and where you are going, by the way, taking the *'road less traveled'* as so beautifully expressed by Robert Frost.

A retreat can take place anywhere, actually. But once you establish an exact place of retreat, the energy builds, creating a vortex where you can immediately go and refresh, realign, and reposition your oxygen mask.

The miracle is, once you begin to retreat to a physical place, the retreat initiates the creation of retreating within (remember *'the kingdom of Heaven lies within'* in the New Testament), a very holy and beautiful shimmering place of Silence that may bring tears of release and relief. A place that may bring lovely laughter again where your joy returns, your retreat can help initiate all of the above, assisting in the beginning of new habits in a new direction, comfortably and safely. Retreats contain our long forgotten spontaneity of our childhood, a wise woman's tool of delight. Do you remember those free-spirited moments?

Imagine a Woman in Love with Herself (Patricia Lynn Reilly) shares with the reader, "A woman's choice to be alone, whether for an hour, a day, a weekend, a month or for a full season of life, deepens her love for herself. In her solitude she reclaims her abundant inner resources, nurtures her original creative spirit, reconnects with her own spontaneity and joy, and remembers her personal dreams and goals."

This is a lot to ponder, isn't it? So breathe into this moment and allow all that has been shared so far to gently wash over you. Note what resonates with you. Put it in a safe place in your heart for later.

Preparation

Come now. Let's prepare for your retreat with me, you dear wise woman. Right now, this very moment! No more excuses. Get out your wise woman tools, the ones you have forgotten. Let me refresh your memory. Some tools are what we loved as little girls. Some tools are what we use now. And, some are what heaven offers us every moment, but have long since forgotten. First, get a pencil and check out this list. Next, check off what intrigues you and what you have available already. Then circle or highlight what you desire to add:

- A rocker with afghan or shawl and pillow
- A candle unscented
- A journal or two, lined and unlined with pens and pencils for writing, crayons and paints, scissors, glue for collage and a small camera for photo journaling
- Something from the earth, ex. pebbles, feathers, flowers or shells
- Something representative of heaven, ex. angel figurine, Bible, cross
- Comfortable, quiet corner inside or out with small table for altar
- Soft meditative music (ex. spa music or Enya) with cd/mp3 player
- Water for hydration
- Your breath
- A special pendant necklace, ring or bracelet, preferably with a semiprecious stone such as turquoise for speaking your truth
- A lightweight carry all bag for your favorite retreat moment items when you travel

You may also wish to have a magazine or book that lends to peace, love and calm, (ex. *Gift from the Sea, Simple Abundance, Spirituality and Health),* a wind chime, lavender essential oil and rosewater for misting, a feng shui placement book, peace lily, place for a nature walk, your favorite tea and teacup.

Letting Go

What you must let go of is phone, tv, radio, computer, gossip magazines, heavy music and noise – no interruptions, including chatting with friends and family. Put it all on the back burner; turn it all off. Schedule yourself and your retreat time into your calendar on purpose daily. Reassign appointments and touch bases, etc., when you return. Remember, this is your oxygen mask time, that crucial, critical moment out of time that brings you to grace.

Time and Space

So as you collect your tools from around the house, yard sales, specialty catalogs and shops, you want to give yourself a couple of weeks to set up your retreat space. (Or not. Once I got started, I couldn't stop myself.)

Learn to move with the energy of it. Allow yourself to be guided as to what goes where. Use a feng shui book (purchase at a half price bookstore) as needed. Placement is important, believe it or not. Play with the feng shui and the bagua for placement. Truly feel the difference. A flow of grace to a correctly placed area calms and also energizes as needed. (Family and friends will notice and feel it, too).

Retreat Without, Retreat Within

Once your retreat space starts creating itself, give yourself permission to retreat, even if all you have is this book, a pencil and a lit candle. Press the "Escape" button, please.

Are you beginning to notice yourself as *Grace in Action* yet? Let's continue.

As you are creating your 'without' space, you will find you are naturally moving to your 'within' space. Lyrics from a lovely song *"There is a Place"* from *Voices on the Wind* by Wild Roses, Beth & Cinde, remind us *'There is a place… come with me... we can go together…stay right where you are… now it's time to start… it's right here in your heart.'* ©1994 Cinde Borup and Beth Pederson (permission granted)

Take a Breath…of Grace

Light your candle; settle into your rocker. Take a new deep powerful breath of life in change with this prayer meditation:

Take a breath of grace in action
A deep breath in this beautiful moment
Allow that sweet breath to flow all the way
Down to the belly.
Now release in tenderness toward yourself…
Relax your forehead… your brow… your ears… your jaw…
Feel your neck muscles release as you give yourself
Permission to caress into your chair.
Take another breath… relax your shoulders… your arms… your hands…
Your belly—just let it hang loose.
Notice as you relax your hips, your buttocks, your thighs, your knees,
Stretch your calves, your ankles, your feet, spread your toes… Release.
Take another breath, and as you release,
Lift the corners of your mouth into a magnificent smile
Silently reflecting on things you are grateful for at this moment…

The sunshine, the breeze, a good friend, a baby on the way, fresh flowers,
A moment out of time in peace.
Remember how very precious and important you are,
For you are 'Grace In Action'!
The world awaits your gifts...

Small But Bold Steps

Reread the statements below, copy them into your Grace in Action retreat journal, then journal the simplest of possibilities for yourself:

1. *"It will be the western woman who saves the world!"*

   Consider how you as Grace in Action may be part of this magnificence.

2. *"When the wisdom of the grandmothers is heard, the world will heal."*

   Check into the grace of your healing wisdom. What may you share out loud?

3. *"We are the ones we've been waiting for!"*

   Look deep into the beauty of who you are as *Grace in Action*. What you offer will affect seven generations, beginning with your children. The world awaits. What are your gifts?

In *Grandmothers Counsel the World*, thirteen indigenous grandmothers come together to share their stories, their wisdom, their prayers and vision for the healing of the planet. A small but powerful book, *The Great Silent Grandmother Gathering*, reminds of the power of silent prayer for peace. As *Grace in Action*, you also have a beautiful and powerful opportunity to make a difference. Lao Tsu has said, "A journey of a thousand miles begins with a single step." Your steps involve grace as you hold that sacred place of peace in your heart, gently, calmly and courageously connecting energetically around the world with other G.I.A.'s. Grands in Action! *Grace in Action*! You can do this! This is the power that moves mountains, like that of the grain of a mustard seed. You are that!

Three Important Questions:

1. Who are you now that you are not who you were?
2. When will you know?
3. What is your next small step to getting there?

Something to Hold On To…

Courage
A kind blessing with quiet eyes of
Strength so
Powerful
It silently and serenely portrays
Honesty as
The simple truth of
Forgiveness
Love
The silent bridge to Heaven's gate
A little laugh

I had it all the time
Courage
—sharon mcwilliams ©2005

Recommended Reading and Listening

Gift from the Sea by Anne Morrow Lindebergh

Grandmothers Counsel the World by Carol Schaefer

The Great Silent Grandmother Gathering by Sharon Mehdi

Imagine a Woman in Love with Herself by Patricia Lynn Reilly

Life's Companion Journal Writing as a Spiritual Practice by Christina Baldwin

The Secret Pleasures of Menopause by Christiane Northrup, MD

Voices on the Wind music cd by Wild Roses, Beth Pederson and Cinde Borup

Notes:

THE PROFESSIONAL WOMAN NETWORK

Training and Certification on Women's Issues

Linda Ellis Eastman, President & CEO of The Professional Woman Network, has trained and certified over two thousand individuals to start their own consulting/seminar business. Women from such countries as Brazil, Argentina, the Bahamas, Costa Rica, Bermuda, Nigeria, South Africa, Malaysia, and Mexico have attended trainings.

Topics for certification include:
• Diversity & Multiculturalism
• Women's Issues
• Women: A Journey to Wellness
• Save Our Youth
• Teen Image & Social Etiquette
• Leadership & Empowerment Skills for Youth
• Customer Service & Professionalism
• Marketing a Consulting Practice
• Professional Coaching
• Professional Presentation Skills

If you are interested in learning more about becoming certified or about starting your own consulting/seminar business contact:

The Professional Woman Network
P.O. Box 333
Prospect, KY 40059
(502) 566-9900
lindaeastman@prodigy.net
www.prowoman.net

Women's Empowerment Series

The Power of Change: Reinvent Yourself at Any Age

Life is an Attitude. The Power of Positive Thinking

Transformation: Reinventing the Woman Within

Learning to Love Yourself: Self-Esteem for Women

A Journey Within: Self-Discovery for Women

The Woman's Handbook for Self-Confidence

Remove the Mask! Living an Authentic Life

The Woman's Handbook for Self-Empowerment

Becoming Your Own Best Friend

The Self-Architect: Redesigning Your Life

The African American Library

Learning to Love Yourself: A Handbook for the African American Woman

Wellness for the African American Woman: Mind, Body & Spririt

Life Skills for the African American Woman

Raising African American Boys

Raising African American Girls

Living Your Vision and Purpose

The Professional Woman Network - Book Series

Becoming the Professional Woman

Customer Service & Professionalism for Women

Self-Esteem & Empowerment for Women

The Young Woman's Guide for Personal Success

The Christian Woman's Guide for Personal Success

Survival Skills for the African-American Woman

Overcoming the SuperWoman Syndrome
You're on Stage! Image, Etiquette, Branding & Style
Women's Journey to Wellness: Mind, Body & Spirit
A Woman's Survival Guide for Obstacles, Transition & Change
Women as Leaders: Strategies for Empowerment & Communication
Beyond the Body! Developing Inner Beauty
The Young Man's Guide for Personal Success
Emotional Wellness for Women Volume I
Emotional Wellness for Women Volume II
Emotional Wellness for Women Volume III
The Baby Boomer's Handbook for Women

Youth Empowerment Series
Raising Healthy Children in an Unhealthy World
The Teen Handbook for Self-Confidence

These books are available from the individual contributors, the publisher (www.pwnbooks.com), www.amazon.com, and your local bookstore by request.